Kefallinia, Greece
History for tourism
An Island for Holiday Dream

Author
Bernard Fletcher

Copyright Notice

Copyright © 2017 Global Print Digital
All Rights Reserved

Digital Management Copyright Notice. This Title is not in public domain, it is copyrighted to the original author, and being published by **Global Print Digital**. No other means of reproducing this title is accepted, and none of its content is editable, neither right to commercialize it is accepted, except with the consent of the author or authorized distributor. You must purchase this Title from a vendor who's right is given to sell it, other sources of purchase are not accepted, and accountable for an action against. We are happy that you understood, and being guided by these terms as you proceed. Thank you

First Printing: 2017.

ISBN: 978-1-912483-48-8

Publisher: Global Print Digital.
Arlington Row, Bibury, Cirencester GL7 5ND
Gloucester
United Kingdom.
Website: www.homeworkoffer.com

Table of Content

INTRODUCTION 1
   ABOUT KEFALONIA, GREECE 1

HISTORY 4

TRAVEL AND TOUR 13
   PLACES AND THINGS TO DO 18
   DROGARATI CAVE IN KEFALONIA 18
   EXPERIENCE KATAVOTHRES IN KEFALONIA 20
   THINGS TO DO IN FISCARDO, ... 23
   BEST MONASTERIES TO VISIT ON KEFALONIA 25
   XI BEACH FAMOUS RED SAND BEACH 27
   GO SCUBA DIVING IN KEFALONIA 29
   FAMILY ACTIVITIES TO ENJOY 32
   TOP BEACHES NEAR ARGOSTOLI 34
   WHAT TO DO IN LASSI 36
   BEST THINGS TO DO IN ARGOSTOLI 39
   ENJOY THESE OUTDOOR SPORTS WHEN TRAVELING TO KEFALONIA 41
   ENJOY HISTORY ON THE ISLAND OF KEFALONIA 44
   WHERE TO ENJOY NATURE ON KEFALONIA 46
   BEST VILLAGES TO VISIT ON KEFALONIA 48
   TOP BEACHES TO VISIT ON KEFALONIA 51
   TAKE A GUIDED BOAT TOUR OF MELISSANI CAVE IN KEFALONIA 53
   ITHAKI - CHARMING VILLAGES AND SITES FROM "ODYSSEY" 55
   BEAUTIFUL MYRTOS BEACH ON THE IONIAN ISLAND OF KEFALONIA 58
   THERE IS MORE TO SKALA THAN JUST SKALA BEACH 60
   ASSOS IS A TRADITIONAL VILLAGE ON KEFALONIA ISLAND 62
   ENJOY MAKRIS GIALOS BEACH ON KEFALONIA ISLAND 64
   KEFALONIA BEACHES 66
   ARGOSTOLI PORT KEFALONIA 68
   KEFALONIA'S BEST BEACHES 69
   THE EAST & NORTH COAST BEACHES KEFALONIA 82
   GETTING THERE 94
   GETTING AROUND AND SEEING THINGS 99
   HIRING SUNBEDS AND UMBRELLAS IN KEFALONIA 103

Eating and Drinking Out in Kefalonia	104
Weather in Kefalonia	113
Winter in Kefalonia	114
Best Time to Visit Kefalonia	116
Holiday Activities	117
Kefalonia Historical Sights	121
Kefalonia Tours	124
Shopping in Kefalonia	126
Kefalonia's Natural Wonders	128
Kefalonia Churches	132
Kefalonia Sports	136
Kefalonia Nightlife	140
Kefalonia' Resort Guide	145
Resort Guide to Lourdas Kefalonia	145
Resort Guide to Argostoli Kefalonia	147
Resort Guide to Lassi Kefalonia	150
Resort Guide to Fiscardo Kefalonia	153
Resort Guide to Assos Kefalonia	156
Resort Guide to Skala Kefalonia	159
Resort Guide to Lixouri Kefalonia	161
Resort Guide to Katelios Kefalonia	164
Resort Guide to Svoronata Kefalonia	166
Car Hire in Kefalonia	169
The Language	170
Money and Banks	172
Local Industry	173
Healthcare in Kefalonia	175
Loggerhead Turtles in Kefalonia	177
Sightseeing	179
Agios Gerasimos Monastery	179
Archaeological Museum	180
Ancient Acropolis	180
Cave of Agios Gerasimos	181
Iakovatios Library	182
Castle of Saint George	183
Castle of Assos	184
De Bosset Bridge	185

DROGARATI CAVE	188
CYCLOPEAN WALLS OF ANCIENT KRANI	189
KATAVOTHRES	191
LIGHTHOUSE OF SAINT THEODOROI	194
MELISSANI CAVE	195
MONASTERY OF ARGILION	196
MONASTERY OF AGIOS ANDREAS	197
MONASTERY OF LAGOUVARDA	199
MONASTERY OF KIPOUREON	200
MONASTERY OF PANAGIA ATROS	201
MONASTERY OF SISSIA	202
MONASTERY OF THEMATA	203
KEFALONIA WILDLIFE	**204**
KEFALONIA VILLAGES	**212**

Introduction
About Kefalonia, Greece

Kefalonia, Kefallonia, Cephalonia, Kephalonia, Cefalonia, Kefalinia or Kefallinia

Kefalonia is spelled differently by most people. The main cause of this is that Kefalonia has had many different conquerors in its past. The most common way of spelling the island's name the last years is Kefalonia, although the Greeks themselves spell it often with two l's. Kefalonia, which is part of the 'Eptanisa' (Seven Islands), or commonly known as the Ionian Islands is situated about 30 miles off the west coast of mainland Greece. Kefalonia's beautiful sceneries are simply breathtaking. From the green mountains and their beautiful valleys to the idyllic bays and their beaches, you will experience a feeling of serenity that is very hard to find nowadays. Kefalonia is still virtually untouched by mass-tourism, which has altered many other tourist destinations around the world.

Kefalonia's beautiful bays & beaches

Kefalonia Myrtos Bay All the bays and beaches on Kefalonia have their own distinct beauty. Some have rough barren terrain and cliffs behind them and others have olive trees as far as the eye can reach. The most beautiful beach and most photographed on Kefalonia is undoubtedly Myrtos Beach which is shown here on the right and on top of this page. Flanked by white limestone cliffs and carpeted in white sand, Myrtos beach is consistently voted by travel magazines and tourists as one of the most beautiful in the world and has won many awards throughout the years for its beauty. Locally in Greece, it has been voted the number one most beautiful Greek beach throughout the last decade. Despite all these breathtaking bays and beaches, the beautiful mountains and valleys and the unique fauna, Kefalonia island has avoided the mass-tourism influx and has succeeded in keeping its tranquility and beauty.

Kefalonia - Rich with Ancient History
Kefalonia island is supposed to owns its name from Kephalos who was the first king of the area, during the Palaeolithic era. According to the locals, this king founded the four main cities of the island which were Sami, Pahli, Krani and Pronnoi, named after his sons. This explains why the island was called Tetrapolis (Four Towns) during this period. Those four cities were autonomous and independent and they had their own regimes and coins. All cities

were built for strategic and agricultural reasons. If you are interested in Kefalonia's history you can visit the Kefalonian history page on this site. When visiting Kefalonia you can imagine how it must have been like many centuries ago, since not a lot has changed on most parts of the island. This is how Louis de Bernieres found his inspiration to write his famous novel 'Captain Corelli's Mandolin', which has also been filmed in Kefalonia in the summer of 2000.

Ideal for singles, couples and families
Kefalonia (Cephalonia) is therefore the perfect holiday destination for single, couples, families and for the newly wed on their honeymoon. Having experienced the beautiful surroundings, the lovely climate and the traditional Kefalonian hospitality, it will make this idyllic island difficult to depart from. Most visitors that have been to Kefalonia (Cephalonia) once, have returned many times throughout the years, simply because there are very few places in the world left like this picturesque and hospitable island.

History

To better understand culture, literature and soul of Kefalonia people, it must be said that being this island a crossroads between East and West, it has inevitably suffered the domination of many western and eastern nations over the centuries.

The experiences of siege, occupation and war, the kidnapping of young people deported and forced to heavy labor as slaves in other countries, and the presence of gentle arts like music, painting, architecture, literature, and dance, have strongly influenced the life of the inhabitants of Kefalonia.

It's widespread opinion that, all over Greece, the culture of Ionian provinces (Corfu, Lefkada, Kefalonia and Zante) is the most sophisticated in relation to art, music, literature and architecture. This is mainly due to the influence of the Venetians, who ruled the area for 300 years.

Kefalonia could be considered as a cultural garden, since it shows traces from all those cultures present on the island throughout the centuries.

Archaeological finds in different areas of Kefalonia gave evidence that the island was inhabited since 10,000 BC, reaching a peak of civilization during the Mycenaean period (1500-1100 BC).

The mythology tells that the young Kefalos, a refugee from Athens, once arrived in Kefalonia and defeated a group of people called Tafi, who lived in the western peninsula of the island, had been controlling the island for a long period of time before becaming the King.

So, he named the island Kefalonia or Cephalonia.

King Kefalos had four children: Pali, Sami, Krani and Proni, who received a portion of the island each, and for a period of time, each of these areas was an independent democracy.

We can still see these names on the map of the island. Krani is the area at the foot of the mountains around Argostoli.

There are a few important historical events from the Roman to the Byzantine period. The most significant event occurred in the period 886-912 AD, when Kefalonia was appointed as the seat of the provincial government of Ionian Islands. From the 1082 A.D. (26 years after William the Conqueror occupied England) until 1479 (13 years before Columbus discovered America), the Normans, thanks to baron Robert Guiscard (from whom comes the name of Fiskardo village), dominated Kefalonia. During this period of history, the island's capital was The Fortress (or Castle) of St. George located in Peratata.

In 1479 the Turks occupied Cephalonia. Twenty-one years later, on December 24th, the Venetians occupied and conquered St. George Castle and ruled the island of Cephalonia for the next 300 years, influencing its culture, architecture and language. During this period, two towns began to develop, Argostoli and Lixouri.

In 1757 the House of the venetian Governor was moved from Saint George Castle to Argostoli, which became the the capital of Kefalonia.

When in 1797 Napoleon abolished the Venetian state it happened that in the following 18 years the island of Kefalonia (as well as the other Ionian islands) passed into the hands of the French, the Russians, the Turks and the British. In 1815, the Congress of Vienna and the Treaty of Paris passed the law that turned all Ionian islands into the "United States of the Ionian Islands", an independent state under the protection of the British.

In 1812, the British government appointed Charles Napier as the civil and military governor of the island. He was who built bridges, roads and public buildings, the most important of which was the Markato in Lixouri. The Markato was the first Courthouse on the island of Kefalonia, with a capacity of 600 people. This beautiful and famous building, a landmark on the island, stood until the earthquake of 1953.

The inhabitants of Kefalonia had to the heart the ideals of American and French Revolutions, which in the long run led to their effective independence and freedom, but in the short term led to political disorders and bloodshed. Three brave men, Elias Zervos, Joseph Manferatos and Gerasimos Livadas, led the revolt of the people against England. Using the persecution, the exile, the imprisonment, and many other means of violence, the British tried to contain the insurrection, but with no results. In 1850, the Queen declared free elections, and the first greek parliament, called Ionian Parliament, was thus formed.

For the following 14 years the Kefalonia people struggled to annex to the unoccupied Greece (at that time some greek regions were still occupied by the Ottoman Empire). Finally on May 21st, 1864, at noon, the British sailed away from Kefalonia, thus realizing the dream of the island to be annexed to Greece. Nowadays the "Feast of May 21" is still celebrated in all seven Ionian islands.

In 1900, Kefalonia played an important role in both the first and the second world wars, but unfortunately it was occupied by the Italians and the Germans during the Second World War. Many villages were bombed, many people were killed or executed, and many families have been destroyed. After the Second World War, the civil war broke out in Greece, causing much more bloodshed and pain. Not long after, in 1953, an earthquake hits the island of Kefalonia destroying 90% of the houses, and plunging the island into economic, social and geological collapse. So many inhabitants left the island minimizing the population.

However, political and social changes took place in the early 1950, allowing the steady progress of the tiller of the soil, so far considered "a kind of servant." This change was made by a law in 1954 which changed the system under which the land should be owned by few landowners who cultivated using slaves.

In short, the law stated that the owner's land should have been divided as follows: the land cultivated by a "servant" worker had to be splitted so that the worker would have received half ownership in that land he had been cultivated. In addition, the law established that the worker had been able to preempt any land the owner wanted to sell. This law has allowed all people, especially the poor and humble, to become financially independent for the first time.

During the dictatorship of George Papadopoulos, in the late 60s, running water and electricity were brought to the island, while in the mid-80s telephone lines were installed in all villages, bringing a better quality of life to residents.

The Kefalonia Massacre: In 1943, on sep 8th, the commander of Italian "Acqui" division (General Antonio Gandin with a division consisting of 525 officers and 11,500 soldiers) that was defending Kefalonia and the Ionian islands, found himself facing the choice to surrender to the Germans or to resist.

Between september 9th and 11th extensive negotiations were conducted between Gandin and the German lieutenant colonel, Barge, who promised the repatriation of Italians who would surrender, and in the meantime continued to attract new troops on the island.

Gandin then asked his soldiers to decide on three alternatives: the alliance with the Germans, the surrender of weapons or the resistance. Through a referendum soldiers unanimously chose to resist. On September 15th, the battle began and lasted until

September 22nd: German bombers decimated Italian troops destroying the city of Argostoli. The Wehrmacht, according to the orders of the Führer, stated that, because of their betrayal, no italian soldier should have been made prisoner.

On September 24th Gandin was shot in the back, while in a school 600 italian soldiers and officers were mowed down by machine-gun fire, and 360 officers were killed in the courtyard of the "Casetta Rossa" (the Red House, a short distance from Argostoli).

In the end 5,000 soldiers were slaughtered (446 were officers) - the 3,000 survivors, embarked on three steamers going to the German concentration camps, vanished into the sea, sunk by mines. In total 9,640 were the fallen, and the Acqui Division was destroyed.

After many decades, in 2006, with a shocking verdict ("In Kefalonia were traitors"), the Prosecutor of Munich filed the case against the only defendant of the massacre who were still alive (and died in 2009 in house in Bavaria at the age of 89 years). He was the former lieutenant Otmar Mulhauser who had commanded one of the firing squads.

Therefore, the trial for the worst massacre of Italian soldiers, made prisoners by the Germans in the Second World War, ended up in nothing. Excluding the "symbolic" virdict inflicted by the Nuremberg

Tribunal to the General Hubert Lanz (12 years, but he served only three) all proceedings that has taken place in Italy and Germany have led to nothing.

Finally, in 2012, the preliminary hearing judge of the military court of Rome indicted the eighty-nine-year old Lieutenant Alfred Stork, who was at that time a mere german corporal of the "Hunters of the Mountains" (Gebirsgjager), and now faces a process (opens Dec. 19) for having "materially participated to the operations of shooting and killing at least 117 Italian soldiers."

A crime that he had confessed, seven years ago in his interrogation, in which he explained that he was one of the members randomly chosen to be part of the firing squad that killed "73 officers", as himself stated.

To kill the remaining of the soldiers was the second squad, commanded by Otmar Muhlhauser, whose process brought to Stork, who refused to repeat his confession in front of the Italian magistrates.

The defendant is accused of the crime of "involvement in ongoing violence and murder committed by military enemies against Italian military POWs."

A crime committed, as Stork said to German investigators, because after breaking the alliance with Germany "Italians were considered traitors. Consequently we had to shoot."

With the indictment of Stork reopens one of the longest and most controversial legal proceedings after the war and for the first time it will not be against senior officers, but against those who at the time were simple soldiers guilty of heinous crimes as their superiors!

Travel and Tour

Kefalonia: The Largest of the Ionian Islands

The Greek island of Kefalonia was all but destroyed by the infamous Ionian earthquake of 1953, also known as the great Kefalonia earthquake. Nearly all Kefalonian buildings were destroyed outside of a small area in the far north. Kefalonia was able to rebuild, and it is now one of the more prosperous and cosmopolitan parts of Greece.

Argostoli is Kefalonia's capital and largest city where you can find the island's most diverse offering of hotels and restaurants. Be sure to taste the two local specialties, kreatopita (meat pie) and crasato (pork cooked in wine). The waterfront is a popular area that features produce and meat markets and plenty of cafes to sit and relax and watch the ships passing by. If you are interested in learning more about the culture of Kefalonia and its history, check out the Historical and Folklore Museum of the Corgialenos Library.

The well-labeled displays in this fine museum showcase traditional clothing, tools, handicrafts, and objects used in daily life across the centuries in Kefalonia. A highlight of the museum is its collection of pre and post-earthquake photographs. The purpose of the museum is to preserve Kefallonioan art and culture.

If you have the time, be sure to take an excursion outside of Argostoli to see the beaches and mountains. The closest beaches are Makrys Gialos and Platys Gialos, 5km south of the city in Lassi. Lourdata is also a good beach that is 16km away that features an attractive expansive beach set against a mountainous green backdrop.

One of the top destinations in Kefalonia is Myrtos Beach, widely considered to be one of Greece's most breathtaking and picture perfect beaches. Visitors admire the white sand and shimmering blue water set between tall limestone cliffs far below. The beach is 8km south of Assos and drives very large crowds during peak tourist season.

Kefalonia is known for its outstanding vintages from the robola grape. The wet winters and dry summers of Kefalonioa are ideal for robola cultivation. Wine lovers may want to stop at one of the robola vineyards on the island. The best-known winery on the island is the winery of the Cooperative of Robola Producers of Kefalonia, located southeast of Argostoli. Here, grapes from about 300 independent growers are transformed into the yellow green robola, a dry white wine of subtle yet lively flavors. The other two well-known wineries of the island are Gentilini, 2km south of Argostoli and Metaxas, 27km south of Argostoli, almost to Skala.

If you enjoy adventures, there are plenty of options. The calm, crystal clear water of Kefalonia is ideal for kayaking. You can paddle down the dramatic coastline, past limestone cliffs, secluded beaches and forests of cypress trees. Sea Kayaking Kefalonia offers a full range of day-long kayak tours with lunch and snorkeling gear, multiday excursions and certified courses. You can also find a variety of hiking, caving, canyoning, jeep safari, or bike tours on the island.

Kefalonia is one of those idyllic Greek islands that never fails to enchant its guests. The biggest island in the Ionian island group, you'd never realize it was so big unless you looked at a map. No matter where you go, people treat you with all the hospitality that the people of Greece have to offer. Although, it is certainly easy to lose track of yourself here. Whether meandering through the countryside, losing track of time while sunbathing, or enjoying a delicious traditional meal, Kefalonia is a place where you can truly get away from it all. Here are some things that you should do while visiting the island:

Beautiful Island with a Turbulent Past

Kefalonia *is the biggest island on the Ionian Sea. However, because of its location, it also has a turbulent past. Today, people are attracted to the island for its gorgeous beaches and diverse geography. Like many places in Greece, inhabitants successfully merge the past with the present to make a culture that is completely unique. It's also known for its earthquakes. The island was also nearly destroyed by a massive earthquake in 1953.*

Because of its location in the Ionian Sea, Kefalonia has had a turbulent past. Groups such as the Normans, Franks, Venetians, and Turks have invaded the island several times throughout history. It was also the home of the Odysseus, the legendary hero made famous by Homer's epic poem, The Odyssey. In modern history, the Axis Powers occupied it during World War II. Today, it's been rebuilt and is an excellent destination for visitors to Greece. Here are some of the essential things to see while there.

Argostili
Argostoli is the capital of Kefalonia and is definitely worth a visit. The city makes for a great place to stay and is in close proximity

of several popular beaches. For example, Makris Galios is only 4 km or so from the city center. There are also several popular sights to see here, such as the Archaeological Museum, which has several archives on display from the Mycenaean period. This is also a great place to shop for traditional Greek products, such as wine. The Vinaries Wine Storehouse, for example, has several wine products displayed and ready for purchase.

Myrtos Beach

This is the most famous beach on Kefalonia. One of the things that make it so popular is that, even though it is within driving distance of Argostili (about 30 km away), it is far away enough from the city to keep the area relatively unspoiled. As a result, the beach is surrounded by beautiful scenery, rather than being part of an urban sprawl.

Enos Forest

Kefalonia is known for its beautiful forests and mountains. The Enos Forest is one of the most beautiful places on the island and is definitely worth a visit during your stay. Mount Ainos is in this forest, and it is the largest peak amongst the Ionian Islands. This forest also holds many unique plant species, which attracts botanists throughout the world. The forest also holds many opportunities for hiking and exploring by foot.

Getting There

You can either reach Kefalonia by boat or by air. There is an airport, which is accessible from Athens and other Greek islands in the area. It can also be reached by boat. The most popular choice is to take a ferry from Piraeus or other islands in the area.

One thing that makes this island appealing is that it is off the beaten path and doesn't get the crowds islands like Mykonos and Santorini experience. This makes it a popular choice for those who want a peaceful, relaxing experience. Sure, there is the chance to experience the nightlife, shop, and eat a great meal. However, the crowd is a little more subdued than it would be in some of the more common places in Greece.

Places and things to Do

Drogarati Cave in Kefalonia

Kefalonia is an enchanting island. Rich with vegetation and sunshine, it is a place with enough nooks and crannies to help you get lost. Since the island is so big, it is possible to craft the ideal vacation. Whether you want to eat a great meal, sit at a beach, or explore the countryside, you can do it all on this island. For those who love natural beauty, it is also possible to visit beautiful places such as Drogarati Cave. Here's more information:

Getting to Kefalonia

It is possible to get to the island either by taking a flight into the regional airport on the island or taking a ferry. The airport is located in the region known as Svoronata on the island and regularly gets flights coming in from Athens and elsewhere in Europe. Ferries regularly come to the island as well from major ports throughout Greece. You can also take a flight from Thessaloniki, and this is a good bet because the flight from that city to Kefalonia is only an hour long. Once you get to Kefalonia, you can make your way to the cave, which is located in a village called Sami.

History of Drogarati Cave

Like many things in Greece, the Drogarati Cave has ancient roots. It is predicted that the cave itself is about 150 million years old. However, it wasn't until around three hundred years ago that the cave itself was actually discovered. Like many places in Greece, Kefalonia is known for having some earthquakes. There was one that took place three hundred years ago, and this particular one exposed the mouth of the cave. The cave was officially opened to the public in 1963. Researchers have consistently been fascinated with this cave and they believe that there are portions of it that we don't know of. They believe that parts of the cave may lead to the sea.

What the Cave is Like

One of the things that makes the cave worth visiting is how interesting it looks inside. Inside the cave there are unique stalactite and stalagmite formations to observe. It's about 60 meters deep, too, so when you're in the cave you have the impression that you're deep into the earth. The cave itself is also incredibly humid and stays at a consistently high temperature, so it is important to be sure to follow all the safety rules when you visit.

Once you arrive at the cave, you will notice that there are two distinct parts. Only a portion of it is open for tourists, likely because of the extreme temperatures in the rest of the cave. The part that you will be able to visit has a long corridor that leads to an area known as the Royal Balcony. Although you aren't able to view the cave in its entirety, you will be able to see enough to give you an idea of what it is really like.

Experience Katavothres in Kefalonia

Kefalonia is one of those islands that is particularly known for its natural beauty. In fact, it's so large, that it is easy to get lost, in a good way. While much of the natural beauty on the island is focused on the beaches, there are other things to discover, as well. In Katavothres, you will be able to witness a truly unique geological occurrence. While on the island, you definitely won't want to miss it. Here's more information:

Getting to Kefalonia

Before you can head to Katavothres, you first need to make your way to Kefalonia. To do this, you can either take a plane into the regional airport in the Svoronata region of the island, or you can take a ferry. From there, you will need to make your way to Argostoli in order to visit Katavothres. Argostoli is about a thirty-minute drive from the airport and over an hour away from Poros, the main cruise port.

About Katavothres

As mentioned above, Katavothres is the home of a unique geographical phenomenon. You'll want to start your journey in Argostoli and from there, you take Fanari Road about three kilometers until you get to the site. Here, you will be able to witness the interesting phenomenon while relaxing in a peaceful setting. Basically, sea water comes through some cracks in the earth. Instead of it rising to the surface, however, the water vanishes without a trace. This is a rare phenomenon, which means that it has intrigued people for quite some time. In the early 1800's, for example, the English used this to help power their corn mills. Geologists have been studying this for quit some time, too.

How the Water Travels

Although this has intrigued people for centuries, geologists have started studying it in the 1960's Geomorphologists from Australia at that time wanted to try to understand where the water actually came from and where it went when it disappeared. These researchers injected a purple-colored dye into the water when it briefly surfaced before getting sucked back into the earth. From this experiment, they realized that the sea water traveled underground, mixed with rainwater, deposited into the sea at the village of Karavomilos, where it went on to the lake at the Melissani Caves. Eventually, the water from these caves empties into Sami Bay. Although we know how the water travels, it is still largely unknown why it actually occurs. This is part of the mystery that draws people to this site.

Because of how intriguing this natural phenomenon is, people from all over the world are drawn here. Not only that, but you can easily make a day out of visiting here. Start your journey in Argostoli and then make your way to Katavothres so that you can watch it. Take plenty of pictures and be sure to explore the natural beauty of the surrounding area, as well. From there, you'll also want to visit the nearby village before heading back to Argostoli.

Things to Do in Fiscardo,

Kefalonia is an island that seems to have a magical quality. It is a large island that has plenty of areas where it is easy to get lost. Whether you lounge on a beach or enjoy the countryside, there will always be something to do. Another great thing to do is choose a village and start exploring, and Fiscardo, a coastal town about 50 kilometers north of Argostoli, the island's capital, should be one of your first stops. Here's more information about what you can do:

Go for a Walk
One of the charms of this fishing village is the fact that there is some great walking here. You can easily pass the time wandering through the streets and exploring the shops, tavernas, and cafes. You can also walk along the water as well as in the surrounding countryside. Fiscardo is in an area that attracts nature lovers, and the hills and forests nearby have trails that you can easily take to explore.

Lounge on the Beach
Since Fiscardo is a coastal village, it makes sense that there are plenty of beaches to enjoy. One of the main beaches to enjoy is called Emblisi Beach and it is located right in Fiscardo. It is considered to be one of the most beautiful beaches on the island. Even if you aren't staying in Fiscardo you'll want to at least head

here for the day just to see the natural beauty. The beach is made up of smooth white pebbles, which means that you'll want to wear a comfortable pair of shoes while walking. It is surrounded by greenery and the beach is on a bay, so this cuts down on the wind. As a result, it is an excellent beach for swimming.

Go Diving
Fiscardo is also a great place in Kefalonia to go diving. There are two diving centers in Fiscardo the Kefalonia Diving Center and Fiscardo Divers. Both are professionals and geared towards beginner and expert drivers alike. You can rent equipment, take a class, and book a tour through both of these centers. Even if you are an experienced, hiring a guide is still a good a idea because they will be able to show you around some of the unique underwater sites that you can see. Sure, Kefalonia is a gorgeous island above the surface, but it is just as stunning underwater!

Visit a Museum
While visiting Fiscardo, you should visit the Nautical and Environmental Museum of Fiscardo. One thing you will notice about this village is that yachting, boating, and fishing, are all popular activities here. At the museum, you will be able to see the nautical history of the area as well as in Greece as a whole. Since it is also an

environmental museum, you will also have some exposure to the history and culture of the environmental issues on the island.

As you can see, there are a lot of things to do while in Fiscardo. When you aren't doing these activities, you should enjoy a great meal and take in all the good things about the culture of Kefalonia.

Best Monasteries to Visit on Kefalonia

When visiting the island of Kefalonia, it is easy to get lost. The largest of the Ionian islands, it can be hard to settle on something to do. With crystal blue waters and lush mountainside meadows, the picturesque landscape is dotted with quaint villages. There are also plenty of historic religious sites and monasteries that may be worth your time. Here's more information:

Agios Gerasimos Monastery
The mountainside monastery honors the patron saint of the Kefalonia. Dating from the 16th century, it is considered a sacred pilgrimage site. Along with its namesake's tomb, the monastery features the cave where Gerasimos lived for five years upon his arrival from Jerusalem. The priory hosts an annual festival that celebrates his work.

Monastery of Agios Andreas

Named for the Apostle Andrew, the Byzantine-era monastery features frescos and paintings, including one of Roxanne, the Greek Romanian princess who chose to become a nun. The nunnery houses other religious icons and artifacts like embroidered vestments, handwritten epistles and the remains of the right foot of the Apostle Andrew.

Monastery of Argilion
Situated atop a hill overlooking the Bay of Simi, the monastery offers incredible ocean views. Two shepherds established the abbey on the site where they discovered a miraculousn icon of the Virgin Mary in the early 18th century. This religious relic is incorporated into a larger image of Jesus' mother revered by locals.

Monastery of Lagouvarda
The nunnery is renowned for the annual appearance in the churchyard of non-venomous snakes with black crosses on their heads. Their arrival each August relates to a local legend dating from medieval times. Residents touch the small reptiles for good luck.

Monastery of Panagia Atros
The oldest monastery on the island, this historic abbey has been rebuilt numerous times. Built during the Byzantine era, the culturally significant monastery sits atop Mount Atros. The trek up

the mountainside offers magnificent views of Poros and its delightful harbor.

Monastery of Sissia
Founded in the 13th century and overlooking Lourdas Beach, the abbey featured frescos and icons from famous artists. The devastating 1953 earthquake that hit the island destroyed the abbey. The ruins are adjacent to a newly constructed monastery.

Monastery of Themata
Dating from 1096, the abbey is one of the oldest religious sites on Kefalonia. Located on the slopes of Agia Dinati Mountain, the monastery is surrounded by a large pine forest. The pristine natural setting affords amazing views of the eastern shoreline and nearby Ithaca Island.

Monastery of Kipoureon
Situated on the Paliki Peninsula, the abbey provides wonderful views of the Ionian Sea and the island's rugged coastline. It is a prime spot for enjoying colorful sunsets. The monastery, surrounded by lush forests of pine and fir trees, houses a collection of ecclesiastical relics and post-Byzantine period icons.

Xi Beach Famous Red Sand Beach

Kefalonia is one of those islands that gets a healthy amount of visitors each year. They're attracted to the beach for a variety of reasons, such as the beautiful scenery. Since it is the largest of all the Ionian islands, it is also easily accessible. It's fun to wander the countryside and enjoy the lush scenery, but the main draw for travelers and locals alike is that the beaches are amongst the best in Greece. Xi Beach, which has a unique, reddish colored sand, is one of the most famous and popular beaches not only on Kefalonia, but in all of Greece. Here are the details on visiting this beach:

Getting to Kefalonia
Before you can lounge in the sun at the famous Xi Beach, you will first need to make your way to Kefalonia. There is a regional airport here that sees daily flights from other airports in Greece as well as from some parts of Europe. If you decide to fly here, the easiest option for you is to first fly into Athens and then take a flight from the Athens Airport to Kefalonia. You also have the option of taking a ferry, and there are many ferry routes that depart from other islands and ports in Greece that will take you to Kefalonia. When taking a ferry, the easiest option is to take a ferry into Poros, which is the main port on the island.

Getting to Xi Beach

Depending on where you're staying on the island, getting to Xi Beach can be a bit of a challenge. It is located about 40 kilometers away from Argostoli and 10 kilometers from Lixouri. If you know that you want to spend a lot of time here, you might consider finding a hotel or resort that is much closer to this beach. However, since it is a major attraction, you can easily find public transportation or a taxi that will take you here.

Why Visit Xi Beach
The main reason why people choose to visit this each is because of the stunning scenery. It is known for the reddish colored sand, which came about because of the geography of the area. There are also some nearby white sand cliffs that are visible from the beach that also add to the beauty. Also, although the beach is popular, it never feels too busy. It is made up of a long strip of sand that spans about 4 kilometers, which means that you can easily find options to get peace and quiet. There are also plenty of nearby services, such as places to eat and find refreshment, as well as sun beds and umbrellas to rent. The water is also calm and warm and great for swimming. It's the perfect beach for families as well, since the waters are so gentle.

Go Scuba Diving in Kefalonia

Kefalonia is one of those beautiful islands where its easy to get lost. As the largest of the Ionian islands, its all too easy to wander the hills in the countryside in search of the perfect Greek experience. While this is certainly a great part of your trip to the island, there is so much more to the place than that. The water surrounding the island is warm and inviting, which makes the beaches a popular spot as well. However, beachgoers only get to experience a small part of the magic of the sea. In order to get the full picture, you should really take the time to go scuba diving during your stay! Here's more information:

Scuba Diving is Popular in Kefalonia
Kefalonia is always listed as one of the most popular places in Greece to go scuba diving. There are several reasons for this but one of the major ones is that the coastline is rocky, which means that there are plenty of nooks to explore. As a result of this, Kefalonia tops the list for scuba enthusiasts, and many travel here for the sole purpose of diving the waters around the island. However, these diving experiences aren't necessarily for diving experts beginners can also take part, as long as they work through a dive center and take plenty of safety precautions. For beginners and locals alike, it also helps to have a guide.

Hire One of the Dive Centers for a Memorable Experience

As mentioned above, working through one of the diving centers on the island is a good idea not only for beginners, but also for experienced divers. Beginners will find them valuable because this will enable them to learn the skills needed to have a successful dive and then have an expert with them every step of the way during their dives. Expert divers will also find them valuable because these dive centers will have excursions to all of the major underwater dive sites and will be able to lead them to all the most interesting spots. Dive centers on the island include Aquatic World, which has programs for both beginners and those with experience, Fiskardo Divers, which are especially known for their environmental awareness, Kefalonia Diving Center, which has courses as well as trips, and Pirate Divers Club, which offers courses as well as equipment rentals. One of these will be sure to suit your needs!

Visit These Popular Diving Sites on Kefalonia
If you do decide to go scuba diving during your tip to Kefalonia, it is a good idea to make sure that you visit all the top dive sites that are available. After all, these are a big reason why Kefalonia is so popular! Be sure to visit the underwater Temple Cave in Fiscardo, the Canyons, the Blue Canyon in Lassi, and the World War II era shipwreck. These are all great choices!

It's true that Kefalonia is a popular spot for divers throughout the world. Once the diving excursions are over, however, you may want to stick around and enjoy the other facets of the island such as the beaches, historical sites, nightlife, and its many restaurants and tavernas. There's something here for everyone!

Family Activities to Enjoy

As the largest of the Ionian islands, Kefalonia seems well suited for families. Packed with resorts, it's a great place to flock to in order to relax with those that you love. The fact that there are plenty of things to do outside of the resorts makes this the ideal spot for people of all ages. Here are some of the best activities families can do on the Greek island of Kefalonia:

Soak Up the Sun at the Beach
There are those who believe that Kefalonia has some of the best beaches in all of Greece. Whether or not you agree with this statement, you can't argue that the beaches here are gorgeous. Because the waters are so warm and calm, this is also a great family activity! People of all ages love spending the day soaking up the sun and splashing in the crystal blue water. Myrtos Beach, Petani Beach, and Kaminia Beach are all particular favorites.

Explore a Cave

One of the things that sets Kefalonia apart from other islands is that there are some stunning geographical features here. The Melissani Cave, for example, is one of those places that visitors love to explore. Your family could easily rent a boat or kayak in order to explore the cave and the lake that is associated with the cave. You also won't want to miss the Drogarati Caves where you will be able to glimpse an underground church.

Enjoy Outdoor Sports
Because Kefalonia is so beautiful, there is no shortage of outdoors sports that you can enjoy here. As mentioned above, kayaking and boating are popular activities. You can also go scuba diving, snorkeling, and even hiking. Even a simple walk along the beach will expose you to some of the most beautiful scenery that the island has to offer. Don't forget to bring your camera!

Go Sightseeing
There are so many wonderful things to see on this island, it can be hard to find just one. Instead of picking and choosing, why not take a tour so that you can see multiple things at once? This is an easy way to get an overview, and the guides will take you to the top spots. You can also visit the specific landmarks, such as Saint George's Castle and the Roman Villa of Scala and take a tour when you arrive. Acting like a tourist is part of the fun!

Browse Through the Shops
No matter where you are staying on the island, you will find that there are opportunities to go shopping no matter where you are. The whole family will enjoy shopping for the items that they will enjoy taking home! Tourist shops are filled with items for people of all ages and larger towns have a variety of different stores and boutiques to browse through. You may even be able to find a toy shop for the kids!

Top Beaches near Argostoli

Kefalonia is one of those islands that people love to visit. On the one hand, there are enough busy tourist resorts to satisfy even the pickiest of beach goers. However, those who don't love the busy tourist areas will also find that Kefalonia has something for them, as well. The island is large enough for people to get lost in. No matter what kind of vacation you choose, chances are pretty good that you'll most certainly want to visit the beach! Here are some of the best beaches to visit if you're staying in the village of Argostoli:

Makris and Platis Gialos Beaches
Although there aren't really any beaches in Argostoli that are an easy walking distance, Makris and Platis Gialos Beaches come pretty close! They are both around 3 kilometers from Argostoli, and since

the two beaches are near each other, you can access both on the same day. If you don't mind walking 3 kilometers each way, you can certainly walk. However, you can also take a taxi or ride public transportation to these beaches. If you know that you want to spend a lot of your time at the beach, you also may want to consider renting your own car. There are also services, amenities, and even tavernas in the area of these beaches.

Xi Beach
Xi Beach is one of the most unique beaches in the Argostoli area since it has red sand. The beach is gorgeous and there are also some services nearby. The red sand makes for some great photo opportunities and the unique claylike sand makes lounging on it especially enjoyable. If you know you love this beach, you may want to consider staying at a hotel right near it rather than on Argostoli.

Lassi Beach
Lassi Beach is one of those areas that has been built up by tourism. As a result, there are plenty of things to do here! Not only that, but it is also close to Argostoli and is only 2 kilometers away from the village. This beach has sand, chairs to rent, and is especially warm and inviting. Those who want to avoid the busy resorts can stay closer to Argostoli and then visit the beach by walking, taking a taxi,

or a bus. Lassi is also known for its beauty and it is a nice spot for lounging and swimming. You'll also want to take plenty of pictures!

Myrtos Beach

Myrtos Beach is known for being one of the best places on the island for swimming. In fact, those who love this beach say that it is the best beach they've encountered in all of Greece! The waters are calm and warm whether you prefer swimming or lounging in the sun on a chair, this beach will become one of your favorites, as well. Don't miss the rocks on this beach, either. They're unique because they are completely white.

What to Do in Lassi

The Greek island of Kefalonia as a whole is a great destination for travelers and the resort area of Lassi stands out from the rest because it is not only beautiful, but there is plenty to do. Kefalonia Greece, itself is stunning and has plenty of mountain ranges and lush green vegetation to satisfy anyone! Lassi is one of the best villages on the island and there is certainly a lot to do.

Here's an overview of some of the things you can do in Lassi:

Makris Gialos Beach

Anyone who has ever visited Makris Gialos Beach knows that it is one of Kefalonia's best kept secrets. It is easy to overlook the beach, as it is nestled behind a supermarket and colorful flea market. However, once guests make a simple turn after passing these two establishments, a brief trip down a rock-lined footpath leads them to the splendor of the beach. Always free and rarely crowded, this beach is a gem you won't want to miss.

Island Bus Tours
Taking a bus tour is popular activity among Lassi visitors as they offer a terrific way to see the island. Guided by knowledgeable tour professionals, the routes typically include a trip through the town of Lassi itself, and then on to see the sights in nearby villages such as Assos and Fiskardo. Tour guides also recommend great stops for lunch or dinner and they'll accommodate whichever one you choose.

Pirate Divers Club
Anyone who is interested in diving should consider enjoying a morning or afternoon at the Pirate Divers Club. On the shore of Lassi, divers can explore all types of marine life in their natural habitat, with experienced guides who always put safety first. This excursion is a great bet for anyone who wants to see caves, reefs,

underwater canyons, sea walls, wreck sites and the spectacular flora and fauna of the Ionian Sea.

Bicycle Excursions
Because of the beauty of the resort of Lassi and its surrounding scenery, bicycle excursions are a favorite among many visitors to this enchanting island. Reasonably priced rentals can usually be found without much difficulty and bicycles for customers of all ages are available. A great way to see the island, bicycle excursions will likely always be popular in Lassi and nearby towns.

Eden Bar
Lassi is also known for its fun and boisterous nightlife, and the Eden Bar is a great place for those who enjoy tasty cocktails, socializing with other visitors and indulging in a vast array of delicious bar snacks. Set in a quaint garden, as its name implies, the backdrop for the bar and lounge are live plants and beautiful, relaxing lights that provide the perfect ambience for guests. In addition, servers are friendly and strive to treat each patron like a part of their own families.

Lassi's rare, natural beauty, friendly residents, and lovely beaches keep visitors returning year after year. Because of the many interesting and enjoyable activities it has to offer, no vacationer will regret a visit to this outstanding area of Kefalonia. You won't want to miss this gorgeous resort location!

Best Things to Do in Argostoli

Kefalonia is the largest of the Ionian islands, but instead of becoming overwhelmed by its size, it's much better to concentrate your travels on one or two distinct places. The whole island is stunningly beautiful and has many places to wander and explore. Whether you trek through the forests or spend the day at a scenic beach, Kefallonia has something for everyone. However, if you would like a more intimate experience, consider using Argostoli, the island's capital, as your base. Here are some things that you can do while visiting Argostoli:

Museum of Archeology
You begin your stay by taking a look at the Museum of Archeology, which is located on Rokou Vergoti Street in Argostoli. This museum features artifacts that were excavated in various sites throughout the island. Since this island was a main player during the Mycenaean Era, most of the artifacts come from that time period. Though the collection is on the smaller side, the museum is informative and does give a nice overview of the history of the

island. Since the museum is on the waterfront, there are also some great views here.

Cultural Museum

If you're still in the mood to visit museums after you're done at the Museum of Archeology, consider walking a few blocks until you find the Cultural Museum! This island has a rich history, including occupation by the British Empire for a time. Many of the pieces in this museum relate to the era when the British were on the island. Evidence of the British involvement with Kefalonia can be found in various places, such as the bridge that connects Argostoli with the rest of the island.

Main Harbor

Argostoli's main harbor is a place where a lot of activity, both by locals and visitors, is centralized. On most Saturdays, the harbor comes alive with a bustling market. There are also plenty of shops to browse in as well as various restaurants, tavernas, and cafes, many of which overlook the water. If you love great food and prefer an area with a lot of activity, you won't want to miss this!

Platia Valianou

Platia Valianou is Argostoli's main square and if you're looking for an alternative to the harbor for places to eat and shop, consider heading here. There are plenty of restaurants and cafes to keep anyone satisfied! Spend some time wandering the streets, looking in the shops, and even eating a great meal.

Beaches
If you love the beach, Argostoli is also another ideal location. There are several beaches nearby, including Makri Yialos and Plati Yialos, both of which can be accessed on food. Spend some time lounging at the beach and then walk to the harbor or main square for a bite to eat after you're done!

These activities will certainly pass the time nicely during your stay in Argostoli and the city does make an excellent location to base the rest of your travels in Kefalonia. If this city looks fairly new, it's because much of the older city was destroyed in a devastating earthquake that took place in 1953, which made it necessary to rebuild much of the city.

Enjoy These Outdoor Sports When Traveling to Kefalonia

Kefalonia is one of those Greek islands that has a rich geography. Because of that and its sheer size, it gives the impression that you can easily get lost here. This also means that there is certainly more to do here than just lounge on the beach! If you're looking for an active way to enjoy the natural beauty of Kefalonia, consider doing one of these outdoor sports:

Explore Some Caves
There are several caves located throughout the island, many of which can be explored. The two most common caves are the Melissani Cave and Drogarati Caves. You can hike through portions of the caves go spelunking, and even go canoeing or kayaking at the nearby lake at Melissani Cave. If you would like to really explore them, you should consider hiring a tour guide to take you through. With Melisanni Cave in particular, the views are spectacular but the water is deep, which means that if you want to explore by water, you need to stay safe.

Take in a Hike
Since Kefalonia is so scenic, it is the ideal place to enjoy a great hike or two. In fact, the hiking trails are so common here that there are those who flock to the island specifically to hike here. Popular trails include the Fanari Peninsula and Argostoli trail, Paliki Penninsula walk, which is also called Sally's Walk, the Agios Fenentes Monastery Walk, the Assos, Fiscardo and Myrtos Beach walk, and the Agios Georgiois & Mycenaean Tombs walk. Of course, there are other trails located throughout the island so you aren't restricted to

those trails. You can also meander through any of the cities and villages on the island.

Go Snorkeling or Scuba Diving
Sure, you can spend your time lounging at one of the beaches. However, there is a whole world underneath the water that you really can't see unless you go scuba diving or snorkeling. Technically, if you have the gear, you can do either of these activities yourself. However, it is much more fun to hire a guide because he or she will be able to take you to all the best spots! In fact, Kefalonia is considered to be one of the best places to dive in all of Greece.

Enjoy a Bike Ride
Kefalonia is one of those islands that you can easily observe by foot. However, that's not the only way you can see it! This is also a great place to take a bike ride. You can go a bit faster than you would if you were o on foot. Simply rent a bicycle when you arrive at the island and start pedaling you can easily explore the villages using it. It is also possible to take a bike tour and have a guide show you around.

While on the island of Kefalonia, you can certainly do all the typical things you usually do on any of the Greek islands, such as visit the beaches and eat the delicious food. However, there is so much more you can do. It is a gorgeous island that is just begging to be explored in different ways!

Enjoy History on the Island of Kefalonia

Although many people trek to the Greek island of Kefalonia to enjoy the beaches and sunshine, you can't help but be exposed to it during your stay. You can easily spend your time driving or walking through the mountainous terrain, lounging in a sun bed at the beach, and enjoying the delicious Greek food. However, it's a good idea to at least have a little bit of exposure to the island's past because without it, you wouldn't be able to enjoy the island's beauty today! Here's an overview of some of the best places to go on Kefalonia to learn about the island's history:

Agios Giorgos Kastro
The Agios Giorgos Kastro is a Venetian castle that sits perched atop a large hill that is near Argostoli and is a fine remnant of the island's diverse history. This castle was actually the home of the island's capital for a total of two hundred years. Although it has long since been abandoned, the castle does remain to delight its visitors. There are also some excellent views here as well as some Byzantine churches to explore as well as some tavernas and restaurants.

Melissani Cave

This cave, which was formed when water entered inside it several centuries ago, is part of a different side of the island's history. In Ancient Greek mythology, Melissani Cave was referred to as the Cave of the Nymphs. Although it has been around for centuries, it was largely forgotten before it was rediscovered by Giannis Petrocheilos in 1951. Now, this is a major tourist attraction and it is possible to take tours to learn more about it during your visit. Artifacts have also been excavated from here that are on display at the Archaeological Museum of Argostoli.

Archaeological Museum of Argostoli
If you love archaeology and are interested in the ancient history of the island, you won't want to miss the Archeological Museum of Argostoli. As mentioned above, the artifacts that were excavated at the Melissani Cave are on display here. There are also other artifacts that were uncovered from excavations throughout the island. Most of them date back to the Mycenaean Era because Kefalonia was an important part of that civilization. You can either wander the halls and observe the artifacts on your own (they are well-labeled) or you could take a tour to get even more out of it.

History and Folklore Museum
The History and Folklore Museum in Korgialenion is another stop you need to make if you want exposure to the history of the island.

The museum's mission is to help preserve the unique art and culture of the Kefalonians. This is the ideal place to observe the icons that the people display in their homes, the unique clothing, and all aspects of their folk culture. It also focuses on the unique cultures between both the gentry and the everyday farm workers.

While on the island if Kefalonia, it is all too easy to spend most of your time at the beach! While the beaches are some of the best in Greece, there is another side of the island. Be sure to spend some time learning about the history and culture, as well.

Where to Enjoy Nature on Kefalonia

There's no doubt that Kefalonia is a stunningly beautiful island. In fact, this is they type of place that people visit in order soak up the sun, clean air, and enjoy it's natural beauty. In fact, it is one of those islands that are ideal for those who appreciate nature. Whether you wander through the countryside, lose track of time on a beach, or explore one of the underground caves, there are plenty of ways that you can enjoy the outdoors. Here's a list of some of our favorites:

Lounge at the Beach
The beaches on Kefalonia are some of the most stunning in all of Greece. They all feature gorgeous, crystal clear water, lounge

chairs, and plenty of sunshine. You can easily spend the whole day here without knowing how much time has really passed! Top beaches include Xi Beach, Katelios Beach, Kimilia Beach, and Dafnoudi Beach.

Enjoy Water Sports
If you love to enjoy the water but don't want to sit all day on a lounge chair, consider participating in some water sports! Popular sports on the island include snorkeling, scuba diving, and extreme water sports such as jet skiing and water skiing. You can also rent a paddle boat, canoe, or kayak and explore some of the gentler waters on the island.

Hike the Hills
Like most places in Greece, there is certainly no shortage of hiking trails. However, the locals don't necessarily consider what they're doing as "hiking" when they use them. For most, walking through the trails is how they get around. However, these trails can also provide endless hours of pleasure for visitors. If you want to hike, consider the trail at Lefka Beach, which will give you stunning views of the ocean, and the Agia Efimia- Drakopoulata trail, which starts at the village of Agia Efimia and takes you to a monastery. You also don't need to take an organized approach. If you simply want to

walk through the hills in order to explore, you'll find plenty of opportunities.

Take a Boat Ride
Another thing you can do while on the island of Kefalonia to enjoy the outdoors is to go on a boat ride. There are several ways you can do this. As mentioned above, you could always rent a paddle boat, canoe, or kayak and explore the waters on your own. You can also take a boat tour, go sailing, or even take a fishing trip!

As you can see, the island of Kefalonia is filled with plenty of opportunities to enjoy nature. Even if you aren't the type to want to participate in outdoor sports, all you need to do is simply stop and gaze at the scenery. Whether you take a simple walk through the streets after dinner or you eat at a restaurant or taverna with outdoor seating, you will definitely find that this is one of the most beautiful islands in all of Greece.

Best Villages to Visit on Kefalonia
In a lot of ways, Kefalonia is fairly similar to other Greek islands. There are beaches, nightlife, great food, and plenty of ways to relax here. This island, however, is also unique and offers the traveler much more than that! As the largest Greek island in the Ionian group, it's easy to get lost here. Whether you're wandering around

the beautiful countryside or lounging at the beach, there is definitely something here for everyone. One of the highlights, however, is to visit some of the island's best villages. Here's a list of the villages you won't want to miss while you're here:

Fiscardo
One of the things that sets this village apart from the rest is the fact that much of it revolves around the private marina where many private boats, such as yachts and fishing boats, are housed. Traditionally a fishing village, your main draw to coming here will be to eat some of the specialty seafood dishes and to take in the view. The nearby island of Ithaca is fully visible here.

Assos
Assos is a picturesque coastal village located about 35 kilometers north of Argosteri, the island's largest city. There are only about 100 permanent residences here in this village, which means that when you visit here, you will be rewarded with a relaxed atmosphere that is away from some of the other, more crowded areas on the island. This is an ideal place to find a quiet cafe and pass the day gazing at the sea.

Sami
If beautiful scenery is what you're after and you only have time to visit one village during your stay, Sami should be at the top of your

list. Many consider it to be the most gorgeous village on the whole island! Aside from being a gorgeous coastal town, Sami is surrounded by some amazing landscape, including rolling hills and stunning coves. It's also fairly bustling and is the second largest port on the island. However, its size of 1000 permanent inhabitants doesn't detract from its charm.

Agia Efimia
If you want to spend some time in a village that is incredibly picturesque, Agia Efimia is the place to be! Most of the village is concentrated around a small bay where small boats, including small fishing boats, are housed. Because of its closeness to the sea, this is another village that is also known for its delicious seafood and amazing views. There are also some nice beaches here, and the streets are especially great for exploring.

Lixouri
If you want a pretty coastal village that is fairly tucked away but still has a fairly good size, consider Lixouri. It's also easy to get here, especially if you are staying in or near the capital city of Argostoli, you can easily take a ferry. It's also a good village to base your trip at, especially if you want to stay somewhere that is bustling but not too large.

While visiting the island of Kefalonia, consider spending some time in some of these villages. If you find one that is particularly pleasing, consider staying in a hotel or resort near one of them so that you can get your fill.

Top Beaches to Visit on Kefalonia

Kefalonia is the largest island in the Ionian group, which means that there are plenty of beaches to enjoy while you're here. During the height of summer, the air is warm and pleasant, and there is a gentle breeze coming off the sea. It's the perfect weather to enjoy the beach! Here is a list of some of the best beaches on the island

Myrtos Beach
If you have time to visit no other beach while here, you'll definitely want to make Myrtos Beach your highest priority. Before you actually arrive at this beach, however, be sure to find a way to observe it from high above and snap a few pictures. The views while looking over it are just as stunning as those you see while lounging on the beach itself.

Antisamos Beach
Are you looking for a beach that is just as stunning as it is relaxing? Antisamos beach is completely gorgeous, and the crystal clear, warm water is one of the highlights. There are lounge chairs

throughout the beach and it is perfect for families, couples, and individuals alike. The beach is surrounded by hills and forests, which gives it a nice, rustic charm.

Petani Beach
This is another picturesque beach that has beautiful, crystal clear water. This beach has both sandy and pebbled areas, which means that you'll want to protect your feet if you decide to walk on some of the pebbles. Relax on one of the lounge chairs or bring a towel and relax in the beautiful sand. This is also one of those beaches that has some nice waves.

Kaminia Beach
If you're looking for a sandy beach that has some nice nearby facilities, Kaminia is the place to be! Whether you want to rent a lounge chair by the water or relax in a nearby cafe, this is the ideal beach to spend some time. This is also a great beach for walking because the pathway is filled with gorgeous wildflowers.

Makris Gialos Beach
This sandy beach is a popular one with locals and travelers alike. There are plenty of sun beds to lounge in and the water is crystal clear. The Kefalonian sun is particular pleasant here, with a nice warm breeze coming off the ocean. The gentle incline of the waters makes it a good choice for those who aren't strong swimmers.

Skala Beach

Don't let the fact that this is a pebbled beach turn you off. This is one of the most stunning beaches on the island! As long as you bring your footwear while walking on the pebbles, you'll have a great experience. Don't forget to bring your camera because the beach really does have some great scenery! The water here is clear and warm. but there are also pebbles in the water, which means that you'll need special shoes when you go in.

Take A Guided Boat Tour of Melissani Cave In Kefalonia

Kefalonia is one of the most beautiful Ionian islands, and it is also the island in which you will be able to find the amazing Melissani Cave.

People come from all over the world to the island of Kefalonia just to see the Melissani Cave. It is easily one of the most beautiful caves in the entire world. You and your guests will be able to take a guided boat tour through the underground lake, Melissani caveas you will learn the history of the cave throughout your journey. If you are interested in Greek mythology, you will be captivated by the Melissani Cave's link to Greek mythology.

The most breathtaking views from within the cave are where there are breaks in the cave above you, and the sun peers in through the holes, and shines down on the bluest water you have ever seen. It really is a fascinating experience, and it almost feels like you are on the set of a Pirates of the Caribbean movie. The best advice that I can give to you is to visit the Melissani Cave in the morning, as that is when the sun will shine the brightest, which will beautifully illuminate the bowels of the cave. As you can imagine, the photo opportunities are aplenty within Melissani Cave. As beautiful as it looks, the water isn't ideal for swimming. With the lake being deprived of sunlight in most areas, the water temperature is noticeably cold.

There are plenty of other adventurous activities to partake in while you're in the area, too. To really get the complete experience of what Kefalonia looks like and what the island has to offer, you can go on a kayaking trip with Sea Kayaking Kefalonia. You can split up the trips that you take with Sea Kayaking Kefalonia over several different days so that you don't miss out on a single thing. A professional with your safety in mind as their top priority will take you to all of the most amazing beaches nearby, and give you a guided tour of all of the different landmarks that you will pass by on your journey. It is an unforgettable experience that will give you a great workout, as well as great memories.

The outdoor adventures don't stop there, though. Outdoor Kefalonia offers a wide variety of extreme sports that will take you to parts of Kefalonia that even the local residents of the island didn't even knew existed. Outdoor Kefalonia will take you off the beaten path and into the beautiful wilderness of the island, giving you an up close and personal experience with the scenic beauty of Kefalonia. You can arrange all kinds of outdoor activities, like hikes, jeep safaris, cave explorations, kayaking, canyoning and rappelling tours and more. For the price, and for the wide variety of services that they offer, you really can't beat it. All of the company's employees are incredibly professional, and take every necessary precaution to ensure that you and your guests have the safest and most memorable experience possible!

Ithaki -Charming Villages and Sites from "Odyssey"

Ithaki is an Ionian island that can be found between Kefalonia and mainland Greece. It's comprised of laid-back villages spread throughout two large bodies of land joined by a narrow isthmus and an unspoiled Greek countryside. Most notably, Ithaki is celebrated as the home of Homer's Odysseus.

Vathy is Ithaki's laid-back main town located on the waterfront. Its central square, Plateia Efstathiou Drakouli, has plenty of cafes and is the only place on the island that has nightclubs, banks, travel agencies, etc. Popular places to visit in Vathy include the Archaeological Museum and the Nautical & Folklore Museum.

Boat tours take tourists from Vathy around Ithaki and to Fiskardo, Lefkada, Atokos, and Kalamos and a water taxi brings beach-goers to Gidaki Beach.

Ithaki's claim to fame is that it is home to several sites from Homer's Odyssey including 4 principal sites:

The Cave of the Nymphs
Located 2 miles northwest of Vathy, this is where Odysseus is said to have hidden the Phaeacians' gifts after he had been brought back to the Bay of Dexia. The cave is locally known as Marmarospilia.

The Fountain of Arethousa
Located 4 miles south of Vathy, this is where Odysseus' swineherd, Eumaeus, is believed to have brought his pigs to drink. It's known today as the spring of Perapigadi.

Alalkomenai

The location of Odysseus' capital has long been disputed by archaeologists. There is no conclusive evidence but Alalkomenai near Piso Aetos is one of the believed locations of the capital.

Bay of Polis
This has been claimed to be the port of Odysseus's capital.

Island Walks offers a guided "Homer's Walk" which explores little-seen parts of the island.

Other villages in Ithaki include:

Anogi
North of Vathy, Anogi is Ithaki's old capital. Highlights of the area include Agia Panagia, a restored 12th century church with incredible Byzantine frescoes and a Venetian bell tower, and Old Anogi, small ruins found uphill from town.

Stavros
Further north from Anogi, this island village is located above the Bay of Polis. Its highlight is a small archaeological museum with local artifacts dating from 3000 BC to the Roman period.

On the slopes of the Mountain of Neion, Exogi offers beautiful panoramic views of the island.

Frikes
Northeast from Stavros is Frikes, the tiny seafront fishing village of Ithaki. This is also the ferry departure point for the nearby island

Lefkada so there are plenty of waterfront restaurants and bars to enjoy.

Kioni
Take a coastline drive south from Frikes to find Kioni. This picturesque seafront village has a small harbor with a few tavernas and cafes frequented by sailors.

Beautiful Myrtos Beach on the Ionian Island of Kefalonia

If you are looking for the most beautiful beach in all of Greece, and perhaps the world, you will need to take a trip to Myrtos Beach 8km south of Assos on the Ionian Island of Kefalonia in the Ionian Sea of Greece. Located in the north-west of Kefalonia, Myrtos Beach has been called "one of the most dramatic beaches in Greece" and has been voted the best Greek beach numerous times and always shows up on best beach lists in travel magazines. It lies between two mountains, Agia Dynati and Kalon Oros, and is one of the most photographed places in Greece.

Myrtos Beach is world-famous because of its beautiful blue and turquoise waters that contrast sharply with the bright white of the smooth marble pebbles of the beach between the limestone cliffs of the two mountains. The beach has a semi-circular shape and stunning scenery. It's a picture perfect beach and the western coast of Myrtos offers spectacular sunset views.

To get to the beach, visitors must go down a steep, winding road about 2km in length from the village of Divarata. On the way to the beach, visitors can enjoy amazing views. During the summer, the Municipality of Pylaros to and from the beach runs a public bus service. It departs from the harbor area in Agia Efimia. Private cars can park in spots at the base of the cliffs.

Because of its beauty, the beach can become extremely crowded in the summer. Beach goers should be advised that the beach drops off quickly and sharply, so the waters might not be the best for small children. The area is also affected by strong winds. The beach has been kept free of watersports and visitors are only allowed to swim in the water. Lounge chairs and umbrellas can be rented on site. A small part of the beach remains completely unspoiled by tourists, ideal for total isolation.

Due to a local ordinance banning permanent structures, visitors looking for dining options will find tavernas at the top of the road leading down to the beach in the village of Divarata where they can also find a beach bar. Nightlife options can be found in the capital of Argostoli.

To get to Myrtos Beach from the mainland, Kefalonia is a one-hour flight from Athens. A cheaper alternative (however longer) is to take a bus from Athens to Patra, the Peloponnese capital, and a ferry to the Sami harbor on Kefalonia's east side.

There Is More To Skala Than Just Skala Beach

On the Ionian Island of Cephalonia, you will find the village of Skala. Despite having a population of less than a thousand people, it is quite the popular travel destination during the summer time in Greece.

If you have the time, take a cruise with Captain Vangeli's Special Cruises. The cruise itself will take up most of your day, taking between seven and eight hours, but it is totally worth it. The cruise takes Skalayou around the island's beautiful coastline, in and out of caves, and making stops in several coves and ports throughout the island. The crew is highly knowledgable and will give passengers all kinds of information in English and in Greek on all of the locations that the cruise either stops at or passes by. Perhaps the most interesting part of the cruise is when you will stop by Navagio Beach, better known as Shipwreck Beach. While seeing the shipwreck is a popular attraction, you will be blown away at how blue the water is.

There are a couple of beaches that you'll want to check out while visiting Skala. Skala Beach is a fantastic beach with its crystal clear water and clean sand, although some areas of the beach have pebbles instead of sand. The water itself is warm, and perfect for snorkeling.

Your other beach option is Kaminia Beach, also known as Mounda Beach. This beach isn't as popular as Skala Beach, because the water is really shallow and folks are unable to go snorkeling here. However, due to its shallow waters, it's perfect for children. In addition to that, the water being so shallow would mean that it's warmer than beaches with deeper water.

The most popular bar in Skala is Akri Seaside Bar, which is a nice little bar that has an excellent view of the water. Come here for drinks, and watch the sunset in an extremely relaxed setting, while one of the best staffs on the island takes care of you. The drinks are cheap, the music is great and the people are even greater.

For a fun day out on the water, you're going to want to look up Dolphin Ski Club. It doesn't matter how old you are or what your experience level is; there is something here for everyone. With the Dolphin Ski Club, you and your group can partake in parasailing, water skiing, jet skiing, fishing trips, snorkeling, boat hire, canoe rental, and even go on a private excursion. The Dolphin Ski Club also offers lessons for beginners looking to try something new. The best part is that all of their services are at affordable prices, and the service is excellent. If you prefer to explore by land which is completely understandable you should check out Makis Scooter Rental. Scooters are great for getting around the island quicker, and this service is top notch with the best prices around.

Suppose you want to see some of the amazing scenery around Skala, but riding a scooter isn't for you give Kefalonia Horse Riding Stable a try! This stable has plenty of wonderfully trained horses, and their horses are ready for riders of any level of experience.

Assos is a Traditional Village on Kefalonia Island

Kefalonia is one of those popular islands that has retained much of its natural beauty. Whether exploring the pristine countryside or spending time at one of the island's unique beaches, the scenery here is part of the reason why people flock here. There are also plenty of villages interspersed throughout the island, and Assos is one of those that you should really consider visiting. Here's more information about this traditional village:

Gertting to Assos in Kefalonia

Assos is located about 20 kilometers or so to the north of Argostoli, which is the capital of the island. Whether you stay in or near Argostoli or prefer to stay closer to Assos is up to you. Typically, most journeys to the island seem to center around the capital since there is so much to do. It should take about thirty minutes to drive from Argostoli to Assos if you begin your journey from there. To get to the island in the first place, you can take either a ferry or an airplane depending on your budget and where you plan to begin your journey.

Why Visit Assos Village

There are plenty of reasons why you should visit Assos village. It is a bit tucked away, which means that much of the tourist crowd might not find their way here. There are only about 100 Kefalonians living here, which means that the village has retained much of its original charm. People pass their days quietly and it is known for being a quaint fishing village. It is also known for being one of the most charming and gorgeous traditional villages on the island and is therefore worth a visit.

What to Do in Assos

Since the village is so small, you may be wondering what you can do when you get here. One of the main draws here is that the village itself is located in a peaceful bay and has a nice waterfront area.

There is also a castle here that originates from the Venetian time period and dates to around the 16th century. Although the castle is in ruins, it is still worth a visit. You can also meander through the streets and visit some of the small shops and enjoy the traditional look of the buildings. There are also some tavernas here where you can eat a delicious, traditional meal.

This is also an excellent village for walking. If you want to see the ruins of the Venetian castle, you will need to take a longer walk, but the path is well maintained and filled with beautiful scenery and vegetation, such as olive trees. There is also a nice view at the castle itself.

Overall, your visit to Assos will be peaceful and relaxing. This is a place for passing a quiet day enjoying the scenery, strolling through the streets, and eating a traditional Greek meal. You won't want to miss the chance to visit this beautiful, traditional village!

Enjoy Makris Gialos Beach on Kefalonia Island

It's easy to lose yourself on Greek islands like Kefalonia. It's not just the sunshine that enchants visitors here. The island is large enough to make people feel like all they want to do is explore everything it has to offer. Whether wandering through the countryside or staying close to the coastal areas, there is something here for everyone.

When people do travel here, they will likely visit the beach at least once during their stay. Beaches like Makris Giolos offer the perfect way to spend your time while on Kefalona. Here's more information:

Getting to Kefalonia and Makris Gialos Beach

Before you can enjoy the beach, you first need to make your way to Kefalonia. Since the island is fairly large, it has both a ferry service and a regional airport. The option you choose will depend on where you originate, your budget, and what type of experience you want. Keep in mind that the ferry is ultra traditional and you will no doubt be amongst plenty of native Greeks as well as tourists while on the ferries.

If you are originating in Athens, however, you might want to consider taking a flight because it is so convenient. Once you arrive on the island, you will want to make your way to your hotel and then later on, to Markis Gialos Beach, which is located just south of Argostoli, which is the capital of the island.

Visiting Makris Gialos Beach

As mentioned above, Kefalonia is an extremely beautiful island that is known for its beautiful scenery. Not only is this beach gorgeous, but it is also conveniently located near the main city of Argostoli, which means that visiting here is convenient. Since it is only 4 kilometers you can easily reach it by car, bus, or taxi. Depending on how close your resort is to the beach, you may even be able to walk if you want to get some exercise. The beach itself is located in an area with plenty of resorts so you might want to stay close to the beach if you know that you want to spend plenty of time here.

Why would you want to visit the beach? First of all, it is located in a gorgeous bay that always seems to have perfect weather. The water is crystal blue and incredibly warm. The sun is warm and seems to shine most of the time. It is also low on wind since the bay shelters people from extreme weather. Lounging in the sun here is a great way to pass the time. The beach also has some facilities to use and there are also chairs and sun beds to rent. If you are staying in a nearby resort, check with your hotel to see if they have a spot on the beach reserved for its guests. Sometimes, resorts provide their guests with sun beds and umbrellas. This is first come, first serve so if your hotel does have space, you'll want to get here early.

Kefalonia Beaches

Kefalonia is one of the larger Greek islands in the Ionian chain that runs down the west coast of Greece with Corfu and Lefkas to the north and Zante (Zakynthos) in the south.

Popularised by the hit Hollywood movie 'Captain Corelli's Mandolin', the island has long been a favourite of the Brits and is promoted by most of the major UK tour operators.

The main holiday resorts stretch along the south-west coast where the best of the beaches predominate. Most of the beaches are big and sandy with shallow water and the usual tourist facilities.

The forest-carpeted mountains offer spectacular views over the island, although drivers face long drives over tortuous mountain roads to reach the more remote northern and eastern resorts.

Car hire in Kefalonia is a must for those aiming to explore the island's attractive, but remote, beaches or planning to visit the Pali peninsula opposite the main port of Argostoli.

Kefalonia is a big island and public transport is relatively infrequent. Consequently most tourists are confined to the south coast with organised day trips to attractions in the north.

As well as magnificent scenery and excellent beaches, Kefalonia also boasts some unusual attractions such as the spectacular caves at Melisani and Drogorati that attract thousands of visitors.

Beaches of Kefalonia
Kefalonia is a large and mountainous island and the beaches are widely spread. The main resorts are at Lassi, Lourdas and Skala - all

widely spread along the south-west coast. Other beaches such as Myrtos and Antisamos are relatively remote and often difficult to reach. The Pali peninsula grows more popular each year but again, it's relatively isolated.

Argostoli port Kefalonia

Once bursting with stylish Venetian mansions and elegant bell towers, bombs were dropped by the Luftwaffe in World War II and a 1953 earthquake reduced much of Argostoli to rubble.

Cement inspired the rebuild and the result is a mish-mash of sober cubes that might be termed 'utilitarian' by the more generous.

Paved mosaics on the harbour promenade emulate waves in a spirited attempt to brighten up a vista of seaside cement and a large grey-flagged square provides city centre focus.

Around the edges of the square are outdoor cafes and tavernas with food of a high standard, if on the pricey side, and if you don't mind scores of squealing children playing football.

The traffic-free shopping street of Lithostroto is mostly department stores and shoe shops and more atmosphere exists in Llandudno, while afternoon siestas turn Argostoli into a ghost town.

Places worth a visit include the Historical and Cultural Museum, filled with memorabilia from the pre-earthquake city when Argostoli was sophisticated, fashionable and a noted centre of culture.

A British-built stone causeway across the lagoon connects Argostoli to the rest of the island.

Kefalonia's Best Beaches

Picking the best beaches on an island that is famed for its hundreds of amazing beaches is no easy task, but there are a few that should be included on every holiday to Kefalonia. The following Kefalonia beaches will appeal to different people for different reasons white sand and clear waters or fun, attractions packed resort beaches, luxury beaches or secluded, stunning shingle beaches. Whatever takes your fancy for the day, you should be able to find in Kefalonia.

Lassi The beaches of Lassi would originally have been considered a part of the Lassi peninsula that encircles the Argostoli bay but now seem to have been swallowed up by the ever expanding Lassi resort. Nevertheless the following beaches, which sit very close to one another are the best Lassi has to offer. Kalamia Beach is the furthest north and offers a thin slice of white sand and a sprinkling of shingle by the water.

It is a stunning setting with gorgeous views of the bay and the white cliffs that surround it. It is reached on foot down a path from the main road and offers sunbeds, umbrellas and a tiny bar that will bring drinks down to your sunbed. Gradaki Beach is all sand and clear waters and is a bit deeper than Kalamia, but is also a bit smaller. The most popular beach in Lassi is Makrys Yialos (or the 'Long Beach') which is just down the main road. Makrys is a beautiful Blue Flag beach that offers golden sand that seems to stretch out for miles. It has all the usual resort attractions and watersports as well as a wide selection of sunbeds and umbrellas, numerous tavernas and lots of family-friendly fun. Finally there is Platys Gialos another Blue Flag winner and one of the best beaches on the island for families.

This is smaller than Makrys Gialos but is an enchanting sandy beach that is run by the council and offers safe, protected fun for the kids. There are toilets, showers, changing rooms as well as snack bars, tavernas, sunbeds and umbrellas. The waters are shallow enough for kids to paddle in (as usual you should never let them out of your sight though) and there is a nice swim for adults that takes you around the rocky headland to Makrys Yialos. In the past the beach even welcomed turtles come to lay there eggs there, though tourists quickly scared them away. (See here for more information about Kefalonia turtles.)

Skala Skala is of course one of Kefalonia's most popular resorts, thanks in no small part to the great beaches. The main beach at Skala is one of the best on the island and offers something for everyone. It is a long sandy Blue Flag beach and though popular, never feels too crowded because there is so much room available. The facilities are excellent for families with all the usual trimmings sunbeds, umbrellas, snacks, drinks and food from local cafes and tavernas on the shore as well as beautiful crustal clear shallow waters for the kids to paddle in.

The setting is picturesque too, with a small but lush pine forest surrounding the beach. For something a bit more secluded and private, Skala also offers the wonderful Mounda Beach. Mounda beach is the place to go for nesting sea turtles in Kefalonia and is consequently one that they are trying to keep tourists from visiting too much. Nevertheless if you are respectful to the environment and stick to the rules it can be a wonderful place to spend an afternoon. That's because the beach is as perfect for humans as it is for turtles offering shallow waters, gorgeous sand and a gentle incline. Clearly there are no facilities yet at the beach but this is a good thing the less development that comes to Mounda the better.

To get there simply walk for about 40 minutes along the coast from Skala Beach.

Lourdas Lourdas beach would normally only be used by people staying in the area; anyone else will need to get there by car. If you are out exploring the island in a car however it is worth stopping off here. Lourdas beach is thankfully free of development and it offers a large stretch of silver-white sand and a sprinkling of shingle. It is quiet, relaxing and with just enough tavernas and shops to keep you busy for an hour or two.

Fiscardo Horgota Beach is the main highlight here in Fiscardo and many people will recognize it as the site of numerous scenes in the movie of Captain Corelli. It is where Mandras is seen fishing out in his boat as well as where he leaves the island from and it is the beach at which Corelli and Pelagia part from one another. It can be reached via the Komitata road and it is worth the trip. It is a simple beach just a strip of shingle and sand but it is beautiful.

Poros Poros Beach is worth visiting not for its beauty or its views but because it offers the best range of water sports on the whole island. This is the beach for a fun day out with the kids and offers everything from waterskiing to jet skiing and from sailing to canoeing, paragliding to snorkeling.

Sami Antisamos beach is to be found a couple of miles to the south of Sami. It is one of Kefalonia's most charming and picturesque beaches with a broad sweep of dazzling bright white pebbles and waters such a shade of clear blue they look like a giant swimming pool. The facilities are limited (a few sunbeds and a bar) but that is what adds to the charm and the seclusion of the destination.

Pylaros Finally, the world-famous Myrtos beach. Of all the fantastic beaches in Kefalonia, Myrtos probably just about wins the beauty prize. Consistently turning up in magazine surveys of the world's best beaches and having been voted the best beach in Greece an astonishing 12 times, Myrtos really is quite special. Perhaps that's because of the constantly changing colors of the shimmering clear water one minute turquoise, the next green, the next dark blue during the day and the contrast between these colors and the smooth white pebbles at the water's edge. Even better still, when the sun sets and drops to the horizon the water reflects back the suns rays and becomes a pool of oranges and reds, yellows and even purple. Throw in the massive mountains overlooking the beach and the steep cliffs to the side and you have a place that is truly wondrous and magical.

Below are Kefallinia Best beaches by their location in more detail!

Beaches on the south-west coast Kefalonia

The south-west coast is the main beach strip of Kefalonia with sandy bays stretching from Fanari, in the north, to Skala on the south-east tip. The main resorts are at Lassi, Lourdas Bay and Skala with small coves between. A good road links them all and this is the place for a multi beach holiday. Other resorts demand long and tiring drives over the central mountains.

Fanari beach Kefalonia

Fanari is the coast road, also called the 'Romantic Road', that skirts the headland from Argostoli to Lassi and it has several beach coves to explore. First out of Argostoli is Maistrato beach, a tiny shingle bay with a small taverna. On the headland is Katovrethes where a restored watermill fronts the famous swallow holes where the sea disappears underground to resurface on the other side of Kefalonia.

Nearby, the picturesque Fanari lighthouse turns out to be only a replica of a rotunda built by the British here in the 1820s.

There are several shingle coves along the shoreline. Near Lassi is a sandy cove at Kalamia, named after the bamboo that surrounds it, with access down a dirt track next to To Psito taverna.

Just before Lassi are small coves of pink sand, sea caves and rocks at Grandakia where a snack bar provides sunbeds. It's a sandy beach with a gentle sea slope and it's much favoured by locals.

Lassi beaches Kefalonia

Lassi is a ribbon of modern tourist development with a string of fine sandy beaches nearby. There is no village, just a narrow road flanked by tavernas, tourist shops and the odd mini-market. The candy coated purple and pink kitsch architecture with its lamp-lit fountains and glass bridges gives Lassi an air of discount Disney.

The inventively named Makrys Yialos (Long Beach) and Platys Yialos (Wide Beach) have fine soft sand and gently sloping shorelines making them great for families with children.

Beach hotels demand an early arrival to nab the best sunbeds and both beaches can be heaving in the high season. There are the usual watersports to entertain and a few rocks to add interest.

Night-life consists of a stroll along the main road or drinks on the terrace of the shoe-box Hotel Mediterranee. Brighter nights are on offer in Argostoli at a more digestible price.

The White Rocks Hotel commandeers a beach at Torkopothiro - just walk through hotel grounds to reach it. The tiny hamlet of Minies has a mini-market, taverna and a good beach, although it's too near the airport runway to be very popular. Next door are the pink sands of Spasmata, separated from Minies by a rock outcrop.

Svoronata beaches Kefalonia

Just south of the island airport is the peaceful village of Svoronata, rather spread out but with a few good tavernas, a mini-market and a garage. The main attraction is a clutch of small beaches and the popular tourist strip at nearby Lassi.

The beach at Ammes is small, narrow and sandy, rarely crowded and with a small cantina. Swimmers must take care as it's noted for strong sea currents. South beyond the cape is Al Helis, is a pleasant secluded bay with pinkish sand, a beach bar and sunbeds at the bottom of steep stone steps.

Around the headland is a narrow sandy strip at Megalipetra, where huge rocks lie offshore, and beyond that Avithos, the furthest and the best, with a long south-facing beach of soft sand, clear shallow seas and a taverna set in the cliff.

The road to Avithos threads through olive groves and the beach itself is well protected by sloping sandstone cliffs. Gently shelving, it offers safe swimming for families while the offshore islet of Dias is topped with a tiny white chapel. Naturists tend to favour the rocky end of the beach as do nesting turtles, so visitors must take care to avoid the nesting sites. A local hotel complex Vigla Natura offers exclusive naturist holidays

Lourdas Bay beaches Kefalonia

The long bay of Lourdas accommodates several beaches. As well as the big, popular resorts there are many small and isolated coves to provide an escape from the crowds.

The small harbour at Spartia has sandy coves each side of the small quay, one of which has rocks encrusted with fossilised shells to make for some interesting snorkeling.

Pessada is the port for the Zakynthos ferry and next to the harbour is a small cove of flat rocks and a small sandy strip below some steep steps. Ferries to Skinari, on Zante, run twice daily in the summer.

Pessada is a pretty village set in a flat plain that offers good walking trails and fine views over the Livatho coastline from the slopes of Mount Ainos. The hillside Divino Winery has guided tours and wine-tasting.

The turning from Karavados leads to a small bay below the village of Agios Thomas where the tiniest of sandy coves has volcanic rock formations and more good snorkelling.

Lithero marks the start of long sands of Lourdas beach, although this end stays empty for much of the season as it is only accessible down a rough track from the attractive hillside village of Vlachata.

Trapezaki beach Kefalonia

Trapezaki is much favoured alternative to Lourdas beach and it's reached down a steep road from the village of Moussata. The road is so narrow that a one-way traffic system operates in the summer.

It has two sandy beaches split by a small marina, where a beach bar opens in the high season. Both beaches are narrow but there is plenty of shade from trees along the shoreline.

The waters are shallow and the sands long enough to ensure they never get crowded. Sheltered by the mountain behind, Trapezaki can feel almost tropical and, being a little off the beaten track, very relaxed and peaceful despite interest from holiday companies.

There are paths and tracks for those who enjoy walking but expect the going to get tough in the surrounding steep hillsides.

Car hire is needed here, although there is a bus service back up the hill that leaves the beach at about 5pm each day.

Lourdas beach Kefalonia

Beneath the towering Mount Ainos a side road drops from the main coast road to the fast growing village of Lourdas where new tavernas open each year as the place garners popularity with holiday firms.

Also called Lourdata, the village square has tavernas and shops set around a huge plane tree and here the road drops steeply to the sea, skirting holiday villas and apartments among the pines.

The long and tiring trek from village to beach results in many holidaymakers hiring a car, which brings plenty of traffic on the narrow country lanes. Lanes and tracks also lead up from the village through dense pine forest and many enjoy a two kilometre nature trail that climbs the hillside to Mount Ainos.

Lourdas' beach of white, sandy grit combines with the neighbouring Trapezaki to create a five kilometre swathe. At the Lourdas end the eye-glaring sand is edged with a grey cement sea wall topped by a dirt track and a handful of tavernas.

Beyond the headland to the south is the cape at Kanastas which is reached by following a rough track from the nearby monastery. Kanastas has a small beach of sand and pebbles but no facilities. Further south still is another dirt track from the village of Thiramona to the quiet, cliff-backed sands at Koroni.

Katelios beach Kefalonia

Katelios, also known as Agia Varvara, has a series of good sand beaches, some favoured by holiday firms and others by turtles.

A small fishing harbour sits at the western end of the main beach, about 200 metres long and backed by eucalyptus and pine with tavernas serving fresh fish.

Sands shelve gently enough into the sea but parts of the beach can attract large gobs of seaweed and the narrow sands slowly turn to stone and shingle.

A large number of apartments have been thrown up behind the sands where a dozen or so tavernas, a couple of bars, some mini-markets and a cash point can be found.

To the east is Potomakia beach where the loggerhead turtles nest. Guided tours of the sands are offered and a trail of blue ribbon leads visitors past the nest sites to the next beach at Kaminia, a pleasant spot with good sands, shallow water and a cantina.

Several beach coves here are collectively called Mounda that end at a cape and even more turtle nesting grounds. Above the beaches of Mounda is the village of Ratzalki now being opened up by tour firms.

Shallow waters make coves along this part of the coast ideal for families, although they are encouraged to stay near the shoreline and away from the turtle nesting sites. Visitors are asked to leave beaches before dusk and members of the Katelios Conservation Group regularly patrol, handing out leaflets to educate visitors on the turtles and their habitats.

Skala beach Kefalonia

The huge sand beach at Skala is long and deep, sweeping around the headland for about four kilometres. Sharp sand and a steep shoreline shelf make it less than ideal for children but the deep sands more than offset any disappointment.

Skala resort has grown fast in recent years and it's now one of Kefalonia's most popular beach resorts. Around 30 tavernas and a scattering of music bars and souvenir shops meet the demands of rising numbers of visitors. Most of the bars and shops are found in the main street or just off it.

Resort pleasures are comfortably low key but there is an open-air nightclub on the Poros road outskirts that attracts the more lively and plenty of island excursions are on offer from travel firms.

For the more culturally minded there are well-preserved mosaics at a Roman villa - look for the signs - and a walk to the old Skala hillside village, demolished in the 1953 earthquake, is popular, although much of the old village has been replaced with luxury villas, complete with tennis courts and infinity pools.

There is a turtle nesting beach around three kilometres along the shore and certain restrictions apply, and which may suit those looking for peace away from the crowds. It may also suit naturists who tend to congregate on the rocky headland and also get to enjoy the best of the sand which shelves more gently into the sea here before giving way to flat underwater rocks.

The east & north coast beaches Kefalonia

Just a smattering of resorts lie along Kefalonia's east coast, from Poros in the south to Fiskardo on the northern tip. A few are in Sami Bay but these are more ports than resorts. This part of Kefalonia enjoys splendid scenery with the island of Ithaka just offshore. The north has mountain trails but little else, apart from the entrancing hamlet of Assos and the jewel of a beach at Myrtos.

Poros beach Kefalonia

The coast road north from Skala gives easy access to a few coves, the most notable being at Heroulaki and Kapri, although neither are anything special. Nor are the beaches around Poros where the ferry docks from mainland Kilini.

Poros has a fine marina, a narrow beach of pebble and sand and a good selection of tavernas. It's a good base for exploring this side of Kefalonia away from the tourist crowds.

The town beach, called Aragia, is a 600 metre stretch of shingle and sand, with a wide, slabbed promenade behind. Sunbeds are for hire but the steeply banked beach makes it a poor choice for children.

Another pebble beach lies across a short river bridge offering more sunbeds, some motor boats for hire and several pleasant tavernas.

A motor boat is needed to reach the few pebble-dashed coves north of Poros with the best at Makria Petra (Greek for long stones) and at Koutsoupia, both of them backed by thick woods of pine.

Antisamos beach Kefalonia

Once a tranquil, rustic hideaway just south of Sami, the photogenic beach at Antisamos was once backed by small fields of grazing goats and attracted the few visitors prepared to attempt the scary descent down a rough track.

But a new road was carved out of the hillside to accommodate movie crews and equipment for shooting scenes for Captain Corelli's Mandolin and now the beach has become a major island attraction.

A large taverna and car park has been built at the back of the beach and cars now make a relatively easy hairpin descent to the dramatic horseshoe bay with its steep bank of brilliant white pebbles.

The beach remains the same sweeping crescent of white stones dropping sharply along an ultramarine shore and framed by tree-carpeted slopes.

But today's growing tide of visitors will find a noisy music bar and ranks of pricey sunbeds.

Sami beach Kefalonia

North of Antisamos, a dirt path off the coast road drops to the picturesque pebble bay at Paliouras where a narrow ribbon of pebble and rock. The main road leads on to the ferry port of Sami, the former capital of Kefalonia and now a fast-growing holiday centre.

Substantially wrecked in the 1953 earthquake, Sami was rebuilt with wide streets and new homes. Some timber houses built by the Danes to house earthquake survivors are still in use but, like Argostoli, much here was lost to the cement mixer.

The resort has a faintly shabby air but this is still a good holiday base, close to the spectacular Antisamos beach and near the island's famous caves at Drogarati and Mellisani.

Narrow and bare strips of shingle and sand line the shore at either end of a promenade that edges a large housing estate.

The road north skirts Karavomilos which has a narrow shingle beach and an attractive water mill. Karavomilos is also the exit point for water that flows into the swallow holes at Katavothres on the other side of the island, near Lassi.

Further north a succession of pebble coves, collectively known as Agia Paraskevi, are mostly reached down short dirt tracks off the main road. A large camping site lies about one kilometre from Sami.

Agia Efimia port Kefalonia

The pretty little fishing port of Agia Efimia (aka Efemia, Effimia or Evfimia) is sited a few kilometres north of Sami. Popular with package tour firms, it is still mercifully free of over-development.

The harbour is one of the departure points for boats to Ithaca and to the mainland port of Astakos. Agia Efimia is also a popular staging post for yachting flotillas and tavernas will often howl to the exploits of holiday sailors. A small selection of tavernas, mostly lined along the harbour wall, generally serve good food.

Agia Efimia suffers from a lack of beaches; just three tiny coves around the resort and a few more scattered along the coast.

Although attractive and with good swimming they are all stone and shingle.

The biggest, Paradise beach (from the taverna of the same name) is just 20 metres long at the bottom of two flights of stone steps. Another secluded beach lies behind the cemetery but the stones here are ankle-breaking in size.

The road north out of Agia Efimia turns inland and, although there are many coves of pebble and shingle between Agia Efimia and Fiscardo, access is by boat or foot only. The most popular are Haglana, Gorgotta and Agia Sofia. South from Fiscardo the nearest are Fold, Evreti and Kakogilos.

Fiskardo port Kefalonia

Touted as a must-see resort on the tourist trail, Fiscardo's building were almost the only ones on Kefalonia to escape the 1953 earthquake, lending a Venetian authenticity to the village not found elsewhere on the island.

A favourite on the day trip circuit - by bus and boat - Fiscardo heaves with visitors at most times of the year, but July and August are a mini-Mykonos of visitor swarms and wealthy boat owners tossing about in the harbour. Expect to have to kill for a waterside table.

For those staying more than a day, the small shingle beaches tucked away on either side of the village are unmapped, unsignposted and without facilities. Embelissi is probably the best, with fine sand turning to shingle, some shade, and some rocky coves to explore.

Kalamaki can be reached by boat and offers fine views to Lefkas while the pebble beach at Dafnoudi is at the end of a narrow gorge near the village of Antipata.

A couple of kilometres along the west facing coast is Alaties, down a narrow lane from the crossroads at Manganos. The tiny beach has little sand but the smooth rocks are ideal for sunbathing and a taverna opens in the summer.

Further south is Agia Ierousalim and a tiny bay of sand and shingle with a summer cantina. The whole area escaped the earthquake and, like Fiskardo, there are occasional but impressive Venetian houses along the narrow lanes.

Assos Kefalonia

The north-west coast of Kefalonia is a rugged wilderness but for the single coastal resort of Assos where an almost unreal beauty stops visitors in their tracks. No beach to speak of, just a few small tavernas perched on the quayside overlooking a small, circular bay but this Greek hamlet oozes a perfectly placid charm.

A spectacularly steep and winding road snakes down into a village tucked neatly inside the narrow neck of a peninsula. The huge rock outcrop is topped with the ruins of a Venetian castle.

The 1953 earthquake reduced the original Assos to rubble, but French funds helped rebuild it in a style largely sympathetic to the landscape, although new houses tend towards the pink and white of toytown Disney.

A narrow pebble and sand strip lines the village square but more attractive and deserted coves lie each side of the peninsula, although a boat is needed to reach them.

Astonishingly, Assos was the capital of northern Kefalonia in 1593 when the castle was built. Today, the fortress is in a state of disrepair but worth a visit for the spectacular views.

It is a tiring walk to the top as cars are no longer allowed. A domed archway splits two kilometres of walls and lead to the ruins of a governor's residence, a barracks and a church.

The fort was once a prison and also the backdrop for almost every sunset scene in the movie Captain Corelli's Mandolin. Assos is also notorious for the German slaying of 1,500 Italian soldiers after Italy surrendered to the Allies in 1943.

A bus runs once a week into Argostoli and there is a local taxi. Boats are for hire and a caique trip to Myrtos runs in the summer. Car hire is recommended for any lengthy stays in Assos.

Myrtos beach Kefalonia

It's the beach all the brochures boast of; Kefalonia's postcard pin-up of Myrtos. Brace yourself for a perilous descent down a gaspingly steep road to a long ribbon of white stones curtained with pale yellow, almost vertical cliffs. It's a gear-screaming journey both down and back up the stupendously steep hill.

Myrtos has won many awards including best beach in Europe. But the scene from the hill above is much more memorable than the hot stone beach below. A flat sweep of white pebble drops sharply into the sea and on windy days the waves can be rough, with several reports of swimmers being swept away.

A basic cafe and sunbeds arrive on the bleached stones in high summer when pale cliffs, white stones and turquoise sea combine to turn the entire beach into a slow roast oven. A small cave at the southern end offers marginal interest and the northern end of the beach is favoured by naturists. A portaloo in the centre is avoided by almost everyone.

South of Myrtos, near the village of Agonas and the start of the Pali peninsula, is the long and little frequented beach of Agia Kyriaki. It's mostly pebble with some sand. There is a small marina with boats for hire, a fish taverna and a summer beach cantina.

Pali peninsula Kefalonia

The Pali or Paliki peninsula lies on the north side of Argostoli Bay, almost another island. Large and remote its resorts are much less visited. Regular ferries run from Argostoli to Lixouri while the road route loops in a long arc north, then south through tiny villages. Beaches on the south coast of Pali are mostly sandy, pleasant and without the crowds.

Starting on the more inhospitable north coast, the delightful Agios Spyridon, is set in a horseshoe bay of sand and shingle. Once a noted smugglers' cove it now attracts those looking for peace and quiet. A blue church perched on high rocks to the west completes the painterly view across Atheras bay while a couple of beach tavernas serve the basics.

There are few roads on the precipitous west coast and Petani is reached by driving direct from Lixouri on a steep and sinuous road. It's a pale copy of its famous neighbour at Myrtos with a 600 metre strip of stone set against sheer white cliffs. Patches of sand dot the steep shoreline and summer cantinas may open.

Near Petani is the pebble beach of Agia Eleni, not so fine, but backed by olive groves and signposted on a rural road from the hamlet of Damoulianata.

Someone has carved 200 stone steps out of the cliff at Platia Ammos, once only accessible only by boat. A strong stomach is needed going down and stronger legs getting back up. But visitors get fine white sand with a little shingle, but the beach is steep and sea currents are notoriously strong.

Lagadakia is a small and charming pebble beach below a lighthouse. It has no facilities but still attracts a fair number of people. Another of the lesser known delights of Kefalonia are the twin beaches in Vatsa Bay. Lesser known because they are notoriously difficult to find.

Good sand beaches called Agios Nikolaos and Akrotiri are split by a rocky outcrop and, at the far end, a stream flows into the sea where caiques tie up to the jetty. Two tavernas open in the high season along with a beach cantina.

Reached by the same road are the village of Kounoupetra and the nearby red sand beach at Mania, once famous for the huge 'moving' rock that often wobbled precariously. It is now stationary, put in its place by an underground tremor. It's still a pleasant enough beach and shallow waters make it good for families. Both come after the Mantzavinata turnoff.

Buying

Local honey - be sure to buy Kefalonian wild thyme honey, it really does taste special - ,and the local wine, Robola.

Souvenirs aplenty, as you'd expect. Some of the jewellery is of reasonable quality and price - you are pretty unlikely to get ripped off on Kefalonia and the Greeks are generally keen to see you get what you pay for in any transaction.

Eating

The Ionian Islands have an own culinary tradition which is quite different from the rest of Greece. It is not influenced by oriental food, but much from the Italian and Austrian kitchen. As many Greeks from the continent moved to Kefalonia after the earthquake of 1953, Greek food is easy to find, sometimes easier than the traditional Kefalonian.

One local specialty is Kefalonian meat pie, available in quite a few restaurants. It's a hearty farmhouse thing rather than haute cuisine. Getting a really good example is not easy, however - the Captain's

Table in Argostoli is perhaps your best bet for this local dish. Food in most establishments is okay rather than spectacular. Menus tend to be the same in most places; its worth tapping into local knowledge about where to eat.

If you're in Argostoli, visit the big bakery on the main street opposite the harbour and buy the little round cheese pies - they're fantastic

There is a lovely cafe/restaurant at the entrance to the Venetian fortress in Kastro, shaded by trees, with very friendly owners - a Greek man married to an English woman (Nicki). The homemade cakes here are delicious.

Moreover, there is a lovely tavern Dionysos in Poros, which a spectacular view to the island of Ithaca and the marina. There you may find one of the most mouth-watering meat pies (kreatopita) in the island, as it is prepared according to a traditional Kefalonian recipe (contains up to three different types of meat). Additionally, slightly exotic scenes in Dionysos are the squids that slowly dry while hanging under the sun, waiting to be fried. Nonetheless, the specialty of the restaurant is moussakas, a small bite of which leaves a mouthful of flavours.

Getting there

Kefalonia Airport

Kefalonia is the largest of the Greek Islands and has quite a large airport that serves roughly 400,000 passengers a year. Kefalonia Island International Airport (EFL) is the only airport on the island and is to be found in Svoronata, nine kilometers from the capital, Argostoli. The airport receives daily flights from Athens (via Olympic Airlines) and takes connections from all over the world. Flight time from Athens is only 45 minutes. You can fly to Kefalonia airport from any of the major UK airports and flights normally depart on Tuesdays, Thursdays, Saturdays or Sundays. The airport has only one terminal that is used both for departures and arrivals and it is, of course, busiest in summer when the charter flights arrive two or three times a day. Flight time from the UK is roughly three hours and fifteen minutes.

On arrival at the airport it is possible to hire a car, or take a taxi or private mini-van into Argostoli, Lixouri or any of the other nearby towns and resorts. If you are heading to Lassi or another resort on a package deal you will probably find that your hotel or tour operator will have arranged a bus to pick you up. If you want to take a taxi into Argostoli it will cost you about 10 Euros. Argostoli is 25 minutes from the airport, Sami 1 hour 15 minutes, Aghia Efhemia 1 hour 45 minutes and Fiscardo 1 hour 30 minutes.

It was announced in 2012 that Easyjet would also be flying to Kefalonia in the peak months (April through October). They now have flights twice a week from London to Kefalonia and they also run an additional service to Kefalonia from Milan from July to September.

Getting Here by Plane

The easiest way to get to Kefalonia is through a package holiday deal that includes your hotels (or villas) and flights (you can find great package holiday deals by using the search box on the right hand side of this site). Most large UK airports have flights to Kefalonia in the summer and they normally leave on Saturday, Sunday, Tuesday and Thursday. Flights take about three hours.

If you decide to travel independently and book everything yourself rather than go through a tour operator (and this is sometimes worth doing because it saves money) then it is possible to book direct charter flights to Kefalonia. Again, these fly regularly from most of the major airports, on the same days as above and can be arranged either online or through your local travel agency.

In 2012 it was also announced that budget airline Easyjet is to begin flights between London and Kefalonia twice a week during peak season (April to October). They will also run a service from Milan to Kefalonia twice a week from July through to September.

Finally there are also two flights a day between Athens and Kefalonia (with Olympic Airlines) if you are flying in from anywhere else in the world or flying to Athens from the UK. These cost 75 Euros and also offer connections to Corfu and Zakynthos.

Getting Here By Boat

Kefalonia, like all of the Ionian islands, is blessed with numerous ferry connections, mainly from Fiscardo to Kefkada, Sami to Ithaki, Patra and Astakos. Poros and Argostoli to Pessadha, Zakynthos, and Kyllini.

Domestic Ferries

There are regular ferry services from Poros and Argostoli to Kyllini. The cost from Poros is about 8 Euros per person or per car. From Argostoli it costs about 12 Euros. There are three or four ferries a day from Poros and one a day from Argostoli.

There is a daily ferry from Sami to Astakos (going via Ithaca) which costs 10 Euros and every other day a ferry to Astakos that doesn't stop at Ithaca (same price.) You can also go to Patra from Sami using the Strinzis Lines ferry (www.ferries.gr/strintzis) which costs 14 Euros per person or car and goes twice daily.

There is a ferry between Argostoli and Lixouri every 30 minutes. It costs 1.8 Euros.

You can sail from Fiskardo to Frikes for about 3 Euros and there are a couple of return trips every day. You can also go from Fiscardo to Vasiliki for 6.4 Euros. You can find the timetable here http://www.fiscardo.com/ferries.htm

Ferries also depart twice a day from the remote Pesada port down in the south of the island to Agios Nikolaos (on Zakynthos) and cost 6 Euros. However you would need a car or taxi at both ends as both ports are quite remote (although there is a bus from Argostoli to Pesada port.)

International Ferries
International cruise ships and ferries come to the Greek Islands from all over Europe and beyond, and the Ionian Islands in particular are a popular destination. The majority of cruise ships to visit Kefalonia arrive at Argostoli or Poros and come down from Italy. Companies such as MSC cruises, Costa Cruises, Oceana Cruises, Princess, Cunard, and Vassilatos all sail constantly around

the Mediterranean between Rome, Venice, Athens, the Ionian Islands and other destinations.

When it comes to ferries there are no direct links between Athens and Kefalonia but there is a ferry connecting Sami with the Greek mainland and Patras. Sami also has ferries departing to Lefkas and Zakynthos, Corfu and other islands and to Italian ports such as Acona, Venice, Brindisi, and Bari. During the high season these ferries depart regularly between Sami and Brindisi, taking about fourteen hours and costing approximately 7o Euros.

Ferry information (and tickets) once on the island can be found at Vassilatos Shipping Company (Antoni Tristi 54, Argostoli 26710 22618) located directly opposite to the port authority in Argostoli and from the Blue Sea Travel Company on the waterfront in Sami.

Getting Here By Bus

There are four buses every day that run between Athens and Kefalonia (going via Patra) and which take one of the many ferries (from / to either Poros, Sami or Argostoli) en route. The bus journey costs about 40 Euros (which includes the ferry) and they all take about seven hours door to door. You can get more information from the KTEL central bus station in Kefalonia (26710 22276/81;

kefaloniakteltours@yahoo.gr). There is also a long distance bus guide here: http://www.athensinfoguide.com/busTT.htm.

Getting around and Seeing things

The bus service on the island is too infrequent to be much use to tourists. Unless you have arrived on your own yacht, in which case you'll have no problem getting to most parts, you need a car or bike if you plan to get around. There are car ferries from the mainland, and many car hire places in towns, though prices vary. Although all travel operators are against motorcycle hire, as long as you have some bike experience, renting a 100cc scooter for the duration of your stay can work out very reasonable. Just make sure you check the bike out before you hire it. Most of the hire places are in Lassi, the main resort, and the capital Argostoli. Taxis are fairly reasonable and individual arrangements can be made with drivers to pick you up at specified times from beaches etc. They are usually helpful and friendly.

> *If you are considering moving to Kefalonia (and most visitors dream about it at least once) there are, unfortunately, a lot of practicalities to weigh up first. More than anything else the current economic hardships the country is going through might give you pause before purchasing a house and moving your life*

over there. But even in more stable times such a move should be considered very carefully. Visiting is one thing, and you can do it again and again, but could you live there in winter when everything closes up and there are only locals around? How is your Greek? Have you stayed there for long periods before or just visited on holiday? Perhaps your best bet is to rent a place for a while and see how it feels to be out there for a long period. If you are still as in love with the island after a winter there, then you can move on to the next step. Those who are considering such a move should start in the south of the island. Houses are cheaper and rentals are easier to find and the main expat community is centered around Argostoli.

Another consideration is whether you need to find work there. Because there isn't a great deal of work going about on the islands. There is occasionally the odd bit of summer bar work and there might be the odd job teaching English as a foreign language but that's about it. Even teaching English doesn't pay that well – most jobs in Kefalonia offer very low rates of pay.

There are a number of expats out there who work online, either freelancing or running their own websites – there is average broadband connectivity in Argostoli and a couple of the big resorts are also connected, but the rest of the island is not ideal *for getting online (although you can get mobile internet connections these days which offer up to about 3mbps). Otherwise moving to Kefalonia probably suits those who have a lot of disposable income and are either retired or financially comfortable. Indeed a residency permit for those arriving without work requires that you transfer a large amount of money to a Greek bank or prove that you have ongoing income of some sort.*

All of this should be weighed up very carefully. More so if you have family. How would the kids feel about moving to another country? How would they fit in at a new, Greek school? When it comes to schools, on Kefalonia a lot of expats send their kids to the secondary school at Keremies (As well as the school in Keremies there is another secondary school in Sami.) You will have little choice in this if you move there – sending kids to school is compulsory on the island and you are not allowed to home school. Primary school begins at six years old in Greece.

Seeing things

The island consists of four peninsulas, and includes some fairly serious mountains, which all goes to make for some outstanding scenery. A series of earthquakes, the last in the 1970s mean there are relatively few relics of antiquity in the island, but architecturally it doesn't look very different from most of Greece. Towards the centre of the island there are two noteworthy caves: the beautiful Drogarati caves seem have suffered somewhat from the loss of rather a lot of its stalactites and stalagmites (allegedly due to occupying German forces using them for target practice during WWII) , but Melissani cave (actually a lake, formed when part of the land above collapsed during an earthquake), filled with brilliant blue water from an underground current which mysteriously flows right under the island, is a memorable experience.

Sami beach (a short drive out of the town of the same name) is also stunning,(blue water, white stones, mountains in a circle around the small bay) but has a permanent traffic jam around it. Myrtos beach, in the West, is also attractive and popular, but can be busy. This beach has a very steep shore break (you are out of your depth about 10ft out!) so is not recommended for non swimmers. Also take plenty of suncream, as the beach is made up of white stones, and in high summer can be blindingly hot. Less ravishing but pretty good beaches which are very much less crowded tend to be found in the south, around Scala and the Lixouri peninsula to the west. The beach of Xi, south of Lixouri, is a lovely sandy beach and always seems to have space and peace. Makris Gialos and Platis Gialos in Lassi are two stunning beaches, but predictably busy. Petani, on the Lixouri peninsula is very pleasant, while Antisamos, near Sami, is where they filmed some key scenes for Corelli. Kaminia Beach is a lovley shallow beach between Anno Katelios and Skala, where you may see a turtle!

Hiring Sunbeds and Umbrellas in Kefalonia

If you're visiting any of the smaller more secluded beaches in Kefalonia then the chances are you'll have the beach to yourself and will have to bring your own deckchairs or beach mats for that extra bit of comfort. However most of the medium to large beaches and almost all of the popular resort beaches will have sunbeds and umbrellas available to hire. In peak season in the resorts you will need to get down to the beach early to guarantee getting a sunbed, as it does of course get very busy. However the rest of the year you will find there are plenty available and you might even get a better deal on price.

When it comes to price, sunbeds and umbrellas in Kefalonia normally come in pairs and the price normally varies somewhere between five and seven Euros in the peak season. Gradakia beach in Lassi for example charges 7 Euros for the pair, Kamina beach charges 6 Euros and Lourdas is the same. As most regulars will tell you, if no one is around you can start using the sunbeds and umbrella and then pay them when (and if) they turn up. Often people don't turn up and you will end up not having to pay anything.

One other thing to bear in mind is that last year only sixteen out of the thirty seven beach concessions on the island for hiring sunbeds and umbrellas had been renewed which left a number of beaches prone to illegal sunbed hirers. Be wary of handing your cash over to just anyone make sure they are the official sunbed concession and that they are not trying to charge you more than 7 Euros.

Eating and Drinking Out in Kefalonia

One of the great pleasures of any holiday to Kefalonia is dining out and watching the locals enjoy their food. Sharing a meal is a great social event in Kefalonia (and Greece) and meals are always a joint effort. No one really orders individual dishes; rather they will sit down together and order an array of communal dishes that will fill every corner of the table. The holiday resorts will offer you all of the usual English dishes but try to avoid these. Greek food is healthy and delicious and there are hundreds of great restaurants and tavernas all over the island that are good value and well worth taking the time to discover. The following is a brief guide to the types of thing you will discover when eating out in Kefalonia:

Breakfast Most Greeks aren't really into breakfast so if you're after a fry up you're stuck with the resorts. A more local diet involves the Greek way of nibbling on smaller dishes and snacks with your morning coffee. This could be anything from savory snacks (such as pies or pretzels) to sweet pastries to local bread. Go to the bakery for bread and try the nine-grain whole-meal breads that are a specialty of the region. Other things to look out for in terms of snack food are pitta filled with various fillings. Pitta that are worth trying include Tiropitta (cheese), Kreatopitta (minced meat), or Spanakopitta (spinach and egg or cheese). A sweet pitta that is delicious is the Milopitta, filled with apple.

Lunch Lunch is the main meal of the day and is later than in northern Europe. Typically it is served between 2 and 3pm and it is essentially the meal that the local chef will put the most effort into, making a full range of hot dishes. (Normally the evening meals will be a selection of dishes that are left over from lunch plus a selection of grilled food you can get cooked on order.) Meals are made up of main dishes and dishes known as Mezedes. Mezedes are a variety of smaller dishes such as saganaki (fried cheese), humus, melitzano salata (aubergine dip), taramasalata (fish, potato, vinegar and oil) and tzatziki (yoghurt, garlic and cucumber), yigandes (white haricot beans in sauce or vinaigrette) and kopanisti (a spicy cheese dip).

When it comes to main dishes it's mostly meat on offer. Popular Greek mains include moussaka (mince with potato, aubergines and cheese sauce), keftedes (meat balls), biftekia (burgers made with fresh mince), chicken cooked on the spit as well as a variety of grills such as pork, veal and souvlaki. Dishes unique to Kefalonia include the Kefalonian meat pie that is a big farmhouse pie (try the Captain's Table in Argostoli for a good example), the local cheese pie, Kouneli (rabbit) and veal with garlic and herbs cooked in wine.

If the beautiful waters of the sea get you in the mood for fish then you need to head to a psaria tavern (a fish tavern) which specializes in cooking fish. Because fish is becoming more and more expensive they price it on the menu by kilogram but you can order as little or as much as you want. Fish dishes on offer include garides (shrimps), barbounia (red mullet) and astakos (lobster). You can also get good kalamari on Kefalonia and it is quite cheap.

For desert there are few options and normally you will be offered a selection of fruit if you are still hungry.

Evening Meal As mentioned above, the main meal of the day is lunch and most of the food for that day will be cooked by local chefs at lunchtime. In the evening Greeks will tend to have lighter, colder food and the usual selection of Mezedes accompanied by some of the grilled mains cooked to order. Dinner is served a lot later than in most northern European countries and it is best enjoyed in summer sat outside under the stars with a cool breeze.

Vegetarian Food in Kefalonia
Greece is not the best place for vegetarians as there is a lot of meat on the menu. But thankfully it is possible to eat well by being selective with the Mezedes menu. Great veggie dishes include the wild greens (Horta), fried cheese (Saga-naki), giant butter beans (Yigantes), fried courgettes (Kolo-ki-thakia), aubergine salad (Melit-zana-salata) and fried aubergine (Melit-zana), to name but a few. The tavern owners are all very helpful and having welcomed tourists for many years most will understand the concept of vegetarianism. Just get to know the phrase 'horas kreas' which means no meat and refer to yourself as a 'horto fagos' literally a 'vegetable eater.'

> *The Ionian Islands have an own culinary tradition which is quite different from the rest of Greece. It is not influenced by oriental food, but much from the Italian and Austrian kitchen. As many Greeks from the continent moved to Kefalonia after the earthquake of 1953, Greek food is easy to find, sometimes easier than the traditional Kefalonian.*

One local specialty is Kefalonian meat pie, available in quite a few restaurants. It's a hearty farmhouse thing rather than haute cuisine. Getting a really good example is not easy, however - the Captain's Table in Argostoli is perhaps your best bet for this local dish. Food in most establishments is okay rather than spectacular. Menus tend to be the same in most places; its worth tapping into local knowledge about where to eat.

If you're in Argostoli, visit the big bakery on the main street opposite the harbour and buy the little round cheese pies - they're fantastic

There is a lovely cafe/restaurant at the entrance to the Venetian fortress in Kastro, shaded by trees, with very friendly owners - a Greek man married to an English woman (Nicki). The homemade cakes here are delicious.

Moreover, there is a lovely tavern Dionysos in Poros, which a spectacular view to the island of Ithaca and the marina. There you may find one of the most mouth-watering meat pies (kreatopita) in the island, as it is prepared according to a traditional Kefalonian recipe (contains up to three different types of meat). Additionally, slightly exotic scenes in Dionysos are the squids that slowly dry while hanging under the sun, waiting to be *fried. Nonetheless, the specialty of the restaurant is moussakas, a small bite of which leaves a mouthful of flavours*

The Cost of Eating Out in Kefalonia

As with all holiday destinations the prices you can expect to pay when you eat out will vary massively depending on where you go. Head to the seafront in one of the busier resorts and you can expect to pay significantly more than a small local taverna in one of the quieter fishing villages. (On the beach you can expect to pay up to 6 Euros for a soft drink and about 20 Euros for a main course if you eat on the beach.) But don't expect the meal to be any better just because it is more expensive. Speak to locals in the area you are staying to get their tips on the best places to eat out on the island. As a rule of thumb however, you can expect to pay roughly the same price in Euros (if they are still using Euros by the time you get there) as you would in pounds for an evening out. Another important rule of thumb is that in Kefalonia (as with many other Greek islands) fish is very expensive so if you are budgeting at all it is probably best to try all of the meat and vegetarian dishes before choosing fish. There are so many to choose from that you could probably have a different main dish every night for a couple of weeks and still not need to order fish.

Another thing to remember is that most restaurants will make you pay a cover charge of one or two Euros. This is for the cost of setting the table and the bread. Many restaurants will also include some oil and vinegar and even a portion of tzatziki.

As a brief guide to prices, you could probably get a Greek salad for 4 to 5 Euros, stifado for about 7 Euros and a large wine for about 2 Euros. A meal for two should be somewhere between twenty and thirty Euros depending on where you eat but there are much cheaper (and of course much more expensive) places. Spend some time searching out the local tavernas in the backstreets and you will be well rewarded both in terms of prices and the quality of the food.

Here then is a very rough guide to the prices you should pay for a meal:

Starters: Basic Dips should cost you about two or three Euros each whilst a hot starter should be somewhere between three and five Euros. The cost of a salad will normally be around five Euros.

Mains: The price of a meat dish will vary greatly but the average price will be somewhere between five and ten Euros. Fish on the other hand will cost you anything from fifteen to twenty Euros.

Deserts: Deserts aren't as popular in Kefalonia as in northern Europe so they will mainly be fruit if offered at all. Expect to pay around three to five Euros.

Drinks and Drinking in Kefalonia

Most locals will drink ouzo with their meals. This is served in small bottles and is normally drunk with water. Another popular drink is retsina, which is a resonated wine and which is not to everyone's taste. Most bars serve a brand of retsina known as Kourtaki, which is the most popular brand, though connoisseurs prefer Liokari or Melamatina.

Most tavernas will have wine lists with all of the best Greek wines on them. These include Domestica, Rotunda, Kambas and Lac des Roches. Kefalonia itself has a long history making wine and is famous for some of its own excellent wines. The most well known appelations of origin are Muscat (a white wine that is very sweet), Mavrodafni (a dark red wine) and Robola (a dry white). The island's main producers are Vitoratos, Sclavos, Soroke, Metaxas, Gentiliini and Divino.

Gentilini was set up over 20 years ago by Nicholas Cosmetatos who was the first to pioneer the fusion of old style wine flavors with the popular western style of wine making. The company led the way for a new wave of Greek and Kefalonian wines which were suitable not just for the palates of the domestic market but also were sophisticated enough for the wider European market. He was soon followed by a number of other companies including one set up by Giannakostas Metaxas, who opened up a winery in 1991 in Mavrata. Aiming for a similar blend of old local cultivars and modern refined tastes Metaxas quickly established themselves with high elevation lower yield vineyards and wines that exhibited a finesse not previously tasted in Greek wines.

If you're not into your wine and consider yourself something of a beer connoisseur then you should try to experience the local brew Mythos beer. This Greek beer has become more and more popular in recent years and has just about caught up to the Dutch beers, Heineken and Amstel which used to dominate. These three will be on sale in most tavernas and you will probably be able to find most of the well-known imports in bottles too. For those of you prefer to drink local when on holiday, there are also one or two other Greek brands such as Fix, Vergina and Alpha, all of which are very pleasant.

A rough guide to the prices for drinks is that soft drinks should cost you a couple of Euros, beers two to three Euros, 500ml of house wine should be around 2 Euros and a bottle of wine anything between eight and thirty Euros depending on the wine.

Weather in Kefalonia

November to March The weather in Kefalonia in the winter is mild on the whole, (though it is still a lot better than the UK winter) with temperatures dropping down to 9c and with plenty of rain. Indeed the island is as beautiful as it is (and covered from head to toe in lush green flora and fauna) thanks to the endless rain that falls in winter.

March to May Spring is a beautiful time to visit Kefalonia. In spring temperatures vary between about 15c and 18c and most days are dry. On the whole you'll see sunshine for about seven or eight hours a day but it wont be too hot. If you are heading to Kefalonia for hiking or biking trips then this is the best time of year to go. There will be April showers, but nowhere near as many as in winter. The evenings are cool (and probably not quite warm enough to sit outside for dinner) though the sea is warm enough to swim in.

June to August In June and July Kefalonia goes fully Mediterranean and temperatures range between 23C and 26c, often going as high as 32c. The weather is constantly hot and sunny (for 12 hours a day), with little rain. There is also very little breeze so it can get very hot always wear your sun cream! The evenings are also hot and it is possible to sit outside and eat until very late at night.

September to October By September the rain is starting to come back though it is still a lovely time of year to visit mostly sunny but cooler (and consequently less tourists.) It's sunny for about seven hours a day and the temperature will average out around 22c. By October this will drop to 18c and there will be more rain still.

Winter in Kefalonia

Most people think of Kefalonia as a summer only destination. That's because in winter it is much more difficult to get there, most of the island closes down (especially in the resorts) and a large percentage of the locals leave the island at the end of the tourist season. This is a shame it might be more difficult to get there and there might be a lot less to do but Kefalonia in winter can be quite beautiful and if you get the chance to go there, it is worth going, if only to escape the rotten weather in northern Europe and the UK.

The weather in Kefalonia in winter is still mild, which makes it a nice escape if the snow and storms are lashing down. That doesn't mean there's no rain in Kefalonia in fact it pours down regularly and heavily, (which is what gives the island its lush flora and fauna) but on the whole the temperature is mild and pleasant. Indeed if you visit Kefalonia for its incredible natural wonders and wildlife there is perhaps no better time to go. There are no clouds and you'll have the hiking and biking trails to yourself. As winter turns to spring things get even better with the arrival of Kefalonia's wildflowers in their hundreds of thousands from the Campanula Versicolor to the Wild Orchid. Indeed at the end of winter the island is covered almost entirely in an explosion of dazzling colors that are worth visiting for by themselves.

This combination of incredible colors and plants, lush greenery and mild climate, not to mention the occasional deposit of snow on the mountain tops and a peaceful tranquility (very few cars, no crowds, hardly any people) is unmatched anywhere else in Europe. Walk around Assos and you won't see another soul, drive through Fiscardo and the few locals you see will nod at you or stop and talk. A small number of locals do still live there and life carries on as normal for them, as they work in the fields or olive presses, vineyards or building sites. But on the whole things are much quieter and fortunately prices are much cheaper. There are still a few places to eat open in Argostoli and Lourdas but they charge a great deal less than in summer. And when you are finished eating you can walk along all of the seafront promenades and harbors and not have to navigate the crowds.

There are occasional events that bring the remaining locals together too, such as the winter open-sea swimming event in Lixouri, (more fun to watch than take part in) and the ex-pat community gets together quite a lot as well. But on the whole winter in Kefalonia is a quiet, reflective experience. The only problem with it is getting there most of the flights to Kefalonia stop at the end of the tourist season and if you do want to get out there it will normally involve flying over to Athens first and getting a connecting flight.

Best Time to Visit Kefalonia

If you're heading out to Kefalonia for some much needed sun then the earliest you should think about going is probably around Easter time. It is possible that even this early in the year you'll encounter some April showers, but once the sun starts shining this is a beautiful time to go there. Similarly, if at all possible you should try and avoid the island from the end of July through to the end of August as this is peak season. During these few weeks you will encounter holidaymakers from all over Europe descending on the island en masse, there will be little available accommodation and the cost of everything will shoot up. Similarly during this period the weather becomes a little too hot and not quite as relaxing.

Probably the best months to visit Kefalonia are May, June, September and October. Prices are a little lower, the weather is just about perfect and there aren't as many people on holiday there. From May the sea becomes that much warmer, the rain seems to arrive less often and the island starts to bloom with flowers and bright green trees. Some nights in May are probably still too cool to sit outside for dinner in a t-shirt, but then again the bars and tavernas are starting to fill up by May and there will be lots going on inside that's worth a look. Some of the beach concessions don't open up until June but again that works in your favor you can normally borrow sunbeds and umbrellas for free when no one is there. Similarly the resort watersports don't normally start up until early June.

The locals will tell you that September is the best month of all to visit the island, with everything open, the weather just about perfect (hot but not too hot with a cool breeze) and the island looking its very best.

Holiday Activities

Blessed with some of the Mediterranean's best and most dramatic scenery, the real highlight of Kefalonia is the island itself. Though gaining in popularity it retains an untouched beauty and a rugged charm that is unmatched by some of the more developed islands. Consequently when it comes to highlights it is really the great outdoors that wins all the prizes. Kefalonia's beaches are some of the finest in Europe and one or two of them consistently win awards and a spot in worldwide best beaches awards (Myrtos Beach is world famous and there are the following blue flag beaches scattered about the islands Skala, Agia Varvara/Katelios, Aragia Porou (Poros), Platys Gialos, Xi? Petani?. But there are other natural highlights too the island's landscape is made up of a series of rolling hills and mountains with lush forests and vegetation filling the vallleys (not to mention the awesome cliffs that tower over many of the beaches.) Indeed Kefalonia's Mount Enos is one of the highest mountains in Greece. Then there are the world famous Melissani Caves on Lake Melissani and the caves of Drogarati, Zervati, the Kounopetra and the Drakospilia Cave in Lixouri. There are the Sakos caves of Skala and the caves at Fiskardo and there is the Koutavos lagoon and the Agios Gerasimos Cave in Argostoli. Other must-sees include the fountain of Karavomylos and a night spent watching the Katelios Loggerhead Turtles, the awesome Poros Gorge and an afternoon spent hiking around Assos, or indeed around any of the villages, so beautiful are the surrounding trails.

Kefalonia's relationship with nature is also responsible for another fascinating highlight of the island its history. After all the earthquakes that have shaken the island on and off for centuries and left much of it in ruins only serve to add to the beautiful and timeless feel of the island. Every village has its own share of ruins and there are numerous fascinating ruins and historic sites to explore, from the Archeological Museum and the Folklore Museum in Argostoli to the Lixouri municipal library (and archaeological collection) and from the Venetian lighthouse and Norman Castle in Fiscardo to the Venetian fortress in Assos to the thirteenth century monastery of Sissia near Vlahata and most famously of all the Venetian fortress at Ayios Yiorios. Take time out to see the Bridge of Drapano and visit the lighthouse of Agioi Theodori, the monastery of Panagia Platitera and the remains of the stone baths in Fiscardo. As well as that, explore the Paleochristian Basilica ruins, the remains of the Roman Mansion and the remnants of the Apollonas Doric Sanctuary as well as the ancient town of Sami. Best of all, take a few hours to explore the hundreds of ancient churches and monasteries that can be found all over the island.

As with most things on the island the churches and monasteries that remain have been affected in one way or another by the 1953 earthquake. Consequently some are still intact whilst others are just a shell, or a ruin of their former glory. Nevertheless as most sit in achingly beautiful surroundings, even the old ruins add to the melancholy beauty of some parts of the island. Religious sites worth checking out include the Agios Andreas monastery, the Panagia Thematon monastery, the Panagia Sission Monastery, the Panagia Atrou monastery (as well as those at Tafion, Koronatou, Kipoureon and Agias Paraskevis) and the churches of Agis Spiridonas, Agia Paraskevi and Prophet Elias.

Other island highlights include tours of the coastline either with a guided boat tour or better still out in your own kayak, wandering the old villages wherever you end up staying and experiencing a vast table full of Mezedes dishes with friends and family in one of the local tavernas, restaurants and cafes. Apart from all the fine food you'll be served at dinner make sure you also get to experience island specialties such as Robola wine, local olive oils and local thyme honey.

Finally no Kefalonia highlights would be complete without the obligatory mention of Captain Corelli and his Mandolin. If you're a fan of the book and managed to sit through the (awful) movie then you'll want to visit some of the places you've seen on the big screen. Most are in Sami, from the Sami town square to the beaches to the winding streets. It's a beautiful place to visit anyway so well worth an afternoon of your time.

Kefalonia Historical Sights

One of the things that makes Kefalonia so beautiful is the mix of stunning landscapes and views with the prevalence of ancient ruins, remains, houses, religious spots, lighthouses and castles. The end result of all of the numerous earthquakes and wars that have hit the island over the years is that the island is a treasure trove for history buffs.

Firstly in Argostoli there is the brilliant Museum of Archaeology that features an extensive and fascinating collection of Mycenean, Roman and Hellenistic relics and treasures that have been found all over the island. Particular highlights include a sculpted disc and plaque that was found in the Melissani Caves (and was thought to be a symbol of a cult dedicated to the god Pan) as well as a 3rd Century Roman head made out of bronze. Next to that there is also the Korgialenos Cultural and Historical Museum that sets out the various artefacts, symbols, weapons and uniforms / dresses of the peoples that have occupied Kefalonia over the centuries. The library was opened by Eleni Kosmetatou in 1966 and contains the amazing collection she put together. There is an incredible display highlighting all aspects of 19th century life on the island that includes near perfectly preserved costumes and lacework, tools and household utensils. Another great exhibit is the folkloric room which highlights all the myths, stories and legends of the island

Another museum that is worth visiting to get an idea of a different kind of history of the island is the Natural History Museum in Davagata. This is only small, but they have managed to make it incredibly interesting and to fit quite a lot in. It details the history of the islands in terms of the flora and fauna found there and outlines the geological timeline.

Other historical highlights on Kefalonia include:

In Fiskardo there is a massive polygonal stonework at the base of the mountains at Pyrgos which was believed to be a Mycenaean stronghold. There is also a unique set of ruins out on the headland of a former Byzantine Church which are particularly beautiful (and unique because they survived the earthquake) and in the south of the harbor another Byzantine church (and monastery) with some beautiful icons inside.

In Lourdas there is the 13th Century Monastery of Sissia that was supposedly founded by St Francis of Assisi and which was home to a large number of talented and intellectual monks and painters such as Tsangorola and Gerasimos Kokkinos.

In Skala there is an entire ruined village up in the hills as well as a third century Roman Villa containing beautifully preserved mosaics and just out of town you will find the ruins of an old Temple of Apollo that have been dated back to 600BC.

Assos is wonderful for lovers of history as it feels like a place from a different era. Dotted all around the village are the well-preserved ruins of the Venetian architecture that was destroyed in the earthquake and sitting above the village is a fantastic looking Venetian fortress. Again, the fortress has seen better days and is now in ruin, but going up there gives a good perspective on the size of the original fort (built in 1584) and offers spectacular views over the island.

There are hundreds of other sites all over the island, from the Bridge of Drapano to the Lighthouse of Agioi Theodori and from the Paleo-Christian Bailica ruins to the Apollonas Doric Sanctuary to the classical Sami village. In Poros there is even an archaeological site of a former mass grave that is believed to be the grave of Odysseyus. So much gold and jewellery has been excavated from the site (now in the Archaeological Museum in Argostoli) that it was almost certainly a burial site for a king and it is now thought that Poros might be the original site of Odysseus' Ithaki, as described in Homer.

Kefalonia Tours

Kefalonia offers some of the most impressive and beautiful scenery of any of the Ionian Islands, and there are so many beautiful beaches and dramatic vistas that it would be impossible to see them all in one day. However, if you are staying on the islands for a week or two and want to spend most of your time sleeping on the beach or by the pool then it is worth taking a tour for a day to get a glimpse of some of the island's best attractions. Tours will be able to take you around everything from Mount Ainos to Lake Melissani to the Drogorati Caves and from the Archeological Museum and the Folklore Museum in Argostoli to the Venetian lighthouse and Norman Castle in Fiscardo to the Venetian fortress in Assos.

There are a number of different tour itineraries you can take, with a number of different companies. Here are a few of them:

Kefalonia in a Day Starting in Skala Square you head out in a coach to the Caves of Drogorati and their fabulous stalactites. From there you move onto the tranquil and eerily beautiful underground lake and the Melissani Cave where you will go out in a small boat and watch the ever changing water colours and more incredible stalactites. After that you'll go on the Fiskardo fishing village for a drink and bite to eat before heading to Agia Efimia port.

Castle and Monastery Tour Spend a day wandering around ruins, old stone castles and monasteries. Starting out in Argostoli your coach will take you to St Georgios Castle, a beautiful Venetian castle with bastions and asymmetrical walls that look out over the sea. From there you'll move over to the impressive Saint Andreas Monastery containing relics such as the foot of Saint Andrew as well as some gorgeous frescoes from the seventeenth century. You'll get a glimpse of the history of the island there too. After that it's lunch in Sami and a look at some of the places that featured in Captain Corelli before driving, in the afternoon, to the famous Monastery of Saint Gerassimos, the island's patron saint, and the cave he lived in for many years.

Yacht Tour In Argostoli and in Fiskardo it is possible to arrange yacht tours of the island(s) for anything up to seven days. You can charter the yachts either with or without a skipper. Make sure the yacht is maintained to the standard set by RYA and Marine Leisure Association. This is a stunningly beautiful way to see the island, though obviously expensive too.

Sea Kayak Tour A cheaper way of getting around the island by boat is to go on one of the sea kayak tours. You can go out for a morning, a whole day or a few days and it is well worth doing, if only to get a different perspective of the island. Paddling around in the gentle and clear turquoise waters that surround the island you can follow a guide through the caves and coves, natural fountains and awesome cliffs that are dotted all the way around. The very best way to see the island. Just make sure your kayak instructor has been certified by an organization such as the British Canoe Union.

Shopping in Kefalonia

Despite the size of the island, Kefalonia only really has one or two commercial areas to do a great deal of shopping. There are however a number of charming little local shops and craft shops in the village and all are worth a bit of your time, both for the friendliness of the owners and because you may well find something in them that you have never come across before. Local goods are on sale almost everywhere and the real highlights to look out for are local craft jewelry in gold a and silver, olive oil, specialist thyme honey and three or four of the local wines. Wines to look out for include Mavrodafni (red wines) and Robola Taoussi (white wines) and the labels to look for include Sclavos, Soroke, Vitoratos, Metaxas, Gentiliini and Divino.

Most of the shops you will find on the island are open 7 days a week although the smaller ones tend to close on Sundays. Shopping hours in Kefalonia tend to be between 9am and 10pm although some of them will close for a siesta in the afternoon, normally between the hours of 2pm and 5pm. Shopkeepers are nearly all fluent in English and are all friendly and very helpful.

The best place for shopping on Kefalonia is the capital, Argostoli. From Valianou Square down and along Lithostrotou Street is the main shopping district for the whole island. Lithostroto street is a busy and long high street that seems to have a shop for just about everything you can imagine, from artisan tradesmen to bakers, gift shops, local fruit and veg grocers, book shops (English speaking), clothes shops, boutiques hairdressers, banks and even tour guides and travel agents.

The resort of Lassi is the next biggest shopping area, though the shops are much more geared towards tourists than in Argostoli. In Lassi you'll find a lot more travel related goods, gift shops, craft shops and supermarkets, all geared towards the summer season. However there are also a number of popular mini markets and craft markets where locals shop and where they sell their own home-made goods.

Kefalonia's Natural Wonders

Kefalonia won the lottery when it came to natural wonders. With more blue flag beaches than any other island and with dramatic coastline at every turn the whole island could be considered a 'natural wonder.' Despite its rising profile though the island is still relatively undeveloped and long may it remain so. Kefalonia has Europe's finest beaches with one of them (Myrtos) consistently coming in the top ten of most 'world's best beaches' awards. Add to that the blue flag beaches of Skala, Agia Varvara/Katelios, Aragia Porou (Poros), Platys Gialos, Xi? Petani? and there is enough to keep you occupied for weeks just in the beaches. But the landscape of Kefalonia is also something to behold, from the mountains and lush hills at its center to the endless forests, vineyards, orchards, caves, streams, fountains and cliffs. You can head out by foot or on a bike almost anywhere in Kefalonia and find some incredible sights. But if your time is short, here are some particular natural highlights worth checking out:

The Cave of Agios Gerasimos and the Katavothres Lagoon, Argostoli.

Just 3 km outside of Argostoli is the Katavothres Lagoon, a fascinating geological phenomenon unique to the area. The name literally means 'the swallowing hole' and the lagoon features a formation into which sea water flows and then drops into deep sink holes. The holes were investigated in the sixties and a purple dye was poured into the holes to see where the water went and revealed that the water passed through a number of underground rivers before re-emerging in Lake Melissani more than 15km away. Two weeks later the same water pours into the sea at the village of Karavomilos.

Whilst exploring around Argostoli it is also worth checking out the Cave of Agios Gerasimos, the patron saint of the island who lived in the cave from 1560 until he founded a Monastery years later in Peratata. There is a chapel inside the cave to this day.

Kounopetra and Draksopilia Caves, Lixouri
If you head about 9km out of Lixouri (south) you'll arrive at Kounopetra, a fascinating geological phenomenon. Sitting out in the middle of the sea is a gigantic rock that was famous for rhythmically rocking back and forth until the 1953 earthquake. It is also part of local folklore that the English tied thick chains and ropes to the rock and tried to move it but failed.

Whilst in the area it is also worth popping along to Havdata and the beautiful views out over the Ionian Sea. Take half an hour to visit the stunning Draksopilia cavern, referred to by locals as 'Dragon's Cave.'

The Karavomylos Fountain, Melissani Lake and the Drogarati Caves, Sami.

The Karavomilos Fountain, near Sami, is the point at which the aforementioned sink-holes from Katavothres Lagoon expel the water that has passed through the underground rivers and lakes. The endless passages and cavities under Kefalonia's limestone rock formations are referred to as the 'Kefalonian Water Mystery' and the Fountain is worth seeing just because it is the end point of the whole process. However, the main natural highlights near Sami are the world famous Melissani Lake and Drogarati Caves. These are the most famous attractions on the island and everyone should see them. Lake Melissani holds the clearest water you can possibly imagine and you can see everything in the deep water below. But as you go out in a boat into the caves you really want to be looking up at the fantastic stalactites on the cave roof above you. Similarly you can walk around the Drogarati Caves featuring long corridors of equally impressive and imposing stalactites. Should you get a chance to go there for a concert in summer, make sure you do the acoustics are amazing.

Turtle Watching in Katelios.
Not only is Katelios one of the island's best spots for hiking and nature walks it also offers the unique opportunity to watch Loggerhead Turtles come onto the beach and lay their eggs. The beach is protected and there is a local NGO dedicated to keeping the masses away from the beach, but you can take part in a nighttime educational turtle-watch if you want.

Poros Gorge
Often called the Araki Gap, Poros Gorge is a massive craggy ravine that drops to a depth of about 80m. It is famous because the islanders believe it was carved out by none other than Hercules. The gorge is supposed to represent the footprints of Hercules after he stood on, and crushed, a mountain that used to be there. The area around the gorge (and around Poros itself) is beautiful too, being covered in lush woods of cypress and evergreens, oak forests and orchards, vineyards, natural fountains and rivers, and flora and fauna of all colors and shapes everywhere you look.

Other natural highlights include the Sakos Cave at Skala, the Fiscardo caves, hiking around Assos and walking around the coast on trails that pass from beach to beach.

Kefalonia Churches

Kefalonia is blessed with a seemingly endless selection of important religious sites, churches and monasteries, some still intact after hundreds of years, many now in ruins. There are hundreds to choose from but the following sites are worth visiting if you only have a bit of time on the island:

The Monastery of Agios Gerassimos

This is one of the most important religious spots on the island as Agios Gerassimos is the patron saint of Kefalonia and they still keep his relics and remains in a silver casket inside the onastery. Gerassimos was a monk from Corinth who founded the monastery on the island in the 16th century and who became famous for his healing powers and skills in dealing with people who suffered from mental illnesses. He chose the site of the monastery, in Omalos near to Valsamata, because it had formerly been the site of a monastery that worshipped the Virgin Mary. He died in 1579 and was later canonized as Saint Gerassimos in 1622.

Today the monastery remains one of the most impressive, and most venerated religious sites on Kefalonia. Nowadays there is a small chapel and the beautifully decorated main church. There is also a cave under the monastery that was built by Gerassimos and it was where he lived for most of his life.

Locals celebrate the 16th August as a feast day for the monastery and their Saint and if you are lucky enough to be around you should take time to watch the procession and the placing of the Saint's sarcophagus under a plane tree shadow and then join in the feasting and dancing.

The Monastery of St. Andreas
The Agios Andreas Monastery (in Peratata) was named after the apostle Andrew and was set up some time during the Byzantine period. It was then taken over by Andrew in 1579 and converted into a small nunnery. After that it was owned and run at various times by a number of local nuns before being gifted a small fortune by a Greek princess Roxanne in 1630 when she escaped there to live as a nun herself.

During the nineteenth century the monastery had a number of run-ins with the British who considered it to be disobedient and who ruined the beautiful frescoes inside as a punishment. Yet it survived to this day and continues to perform holy mass every week, whilst the nuns who live there spend their days working on crafts, robes and gardening. It is a beautiful place to visit and next to the Monastery is one of the few churches to survive the 1953 earthquake. There are some incredible treasures in the museum, from the foot of St Andrew to Priest Basia's shirt, and from two epistles handwritten bu Saint Kosmas Aetelos to the hieratic sceptre and chalice of Nicodemus II of Metaxas and the shroud of Gregorios the Fifth, a national martyr and the patriarch of Constantinople. As well as all these artefacts there are some beautiful frescoes, wall paintings and icons and the famous painting of Romila and her parents.

Atros Monastery

The Atros Monastery is the oldest monastery on the island and is something of a survivor. Since it was first built in the 8th century, during the Byzantine era it has been destroyed an incredible seventeen different times through wars, earthquakes and fires (and has been attacked by everyone from the Saracens to the Nazis) but every time it gets knocked down, the monks simply rebuild it. It sits atop Mt. Atros at about 770m above sea level and is to be found roughly five miles outside of Poros. It is known sometimes as the Theotokos Monastery and other times as the Monastery of Panagia Atrou and it has been dedicated to the birth of the Virgin Mary. There is still an old medieval tower there as well as the 'archodariki' and a Welcome Hall. There is a celebration on the 8th September and a special service the day before. Currently only one monk lives there. It is a must-see even if you don't have any interest in the history of the place and all the artifacts, it is still one of the best walks on Kefalonia, with incredible views of Poros harbor.

Agrilion Monastery

Agrilion Monastery overlooks Sami village and was built in the 18th century on a site dedicated to the icon of Agios Theotokos. It is believed the icon was discovered there by two shepherds who immediately converted and dedicated their lives to the nearby monastery. The monastery itself is now dedicated to the Hyperayia Theotokos.

The Monastery of Sissia

The Monastery of Sissia has looked down over Lourdas Beach since the 13th century when it was founded by Saint Francis of Assisi. It has always been known as a wealthy and influential monastery, and throughout its history has produced talented and intellectual monks and painters such as Tsangorolo and Gerasimos Kokkinos. During the medieval era all of its icons and frescoes were painted by world-famous iconographers and the monastery became so famous that in 1676 a yearly march was introduced by the Venetians that went from the Castle of Saint George to the Sissia Monastery to celebrate St Mark's Feast. The monastery started out as Catholic but gradually became Orthodox. It was completely wiped out by the 1953 earthquake at which time a new monastery was built next to the ruins (which remain to this day.)

The Monastery of Kipoureon

15km outside of Lixouri in the Paliki peninsula is the magnificent Monastery of Kipoureon. It was founded in the late 16th century by Chrysanthos Petropoulos, the Archbishop of Paxi and is referred to as the Monastery of Gardens because of all the various gardens there from which the monks would make their living. Nowadays there is just one monk living there and he welcomes all visitors every day. There is a fantastic collection of Byzantine icons and ecclesiastical relics and treasures inside and though many of the gardens are gone there are still beautiful grounds surrounding the monastery and a thick border of pine and fur trees. Best of all though are the views out over the island (and the jagged, thrilling coastline below) to the Ionian sea and if you get the chance to head there in the afternoon make sure you wait around for the sunset. It is quite special.

Kefalonia Sports

Kefalonia is a tranquil and quiet island so it is not somewhere you would identify as an extreme sports destination. However, for those of you who want to get out and about rather than lying down on a sun bed all day, there is plenty to keep you occupied.

Hiking in Kefalonia

For hikers there are endless trails on the outskirts of all the resorts and villages and it is possible to get a map from your resort detailing most of these. You could spend weeks hiking in Kefalonia up the mountains and through the valleys, wandering through lush olive and orange groves and endless orchards down cliff paths to endless white sandy beaches and still not see everything. Similarly if you wanted to hire a bike (or take your own bike with you) you'll find no shortage of stunning rides around the island. Cycling out from most villages and towns will allow you to see parts of the island that most holidaymakers don't get to see. Riding along the small island lanes you'll pass through endless sleepy hamlets and tiny villages, olive tree lined winding roads and countless melancholic ruins left by the numerous earthquakes and wars.

Watersports in Kefalonia

For those who are after watersports, the resorts are the best options. On the beaches in Skala and other places you'll be able to indulge in paragliding and jet-skiing, parasailing and windsurfing. Kefalonia also offers a number of stranger watersports. There is the banana a large inflatable tube that up to 12 people can sit on (and try to stay on) as it is towed around the bay by speedboat. Kneeboarding is another new one, using a board in the waves that has been designed for you to kneel on as you try and side-slide through the water. Wakeboarding is a cross between snowboarding and surfing and finally there is Oxoon, a hydrojet ski that looks just like a dolphin.

Sea Kayaking
One of the water focused highlights of Kefalonia's outdoor activities is sea kayaking. So beautiful are the bays and coves, the long undisturbed beaches and clear blue waters that going out in a kayak to see the island is a truly beautiful experience. There are a number of kayaking companies on Kefalonia, mostly based in Argostoli and Skala. Make sure you pick one that has qualified instructors, preferably with the BCU qualification. If you can, spend a day or two exploring the calm and beautiful waters and following the picturesque coastline.

Golf in Kefalonia
Unlike many holiday destinations Kefalonia is not famous for its golf and there are no golf resorts or even professional golf courses. Most people will tell you that the reason they return again and again to Kefalonia is because it has not (so far) developed into the sort of place that might have an 18 hole golf course!

If you absolutely, positively can't live without golf while you are away there is at least an 18 hole mini-golf course in the peninsula of Palliki, between Lixouri and Xi beach.

Fishing in Kefalonia
Fishing in Greece hasn't got the greatest reputation simply because the waters have been so overfished by commercial fishing vessels that sometimes it seems like there is hardly anything left in the water. However, it is possible to catch fish from time to time and there are few more enchanting places in the world to sit and wile away the hours than Kefalonia. The best month for fishing is September when there are a few migrating fish passing through. These include a number of larger species as well as sea bass and big snapper.

If you want to fish from a boat in Kefalonia you'll need to get a license from one of the harbor towns but if you're happy to just fish on the rocks, on a beach or in one of the harbors then it is free. There are bait shops in both Poros and Argostoli and you can fish in both places. In Poros there is a pier that the locals all use and there are numerous popular spots in Argostoli. In Skala there is a spot to the right of the beach (when facing out to sea) on the rocks that has long been popular with local residents.

Supposedly the most successful method of fishing in these parts is float fishing, leaving the bait to sit just above the weeds from the beach.

Kefalonia Nightlife

Because it is such a beautifully tranquil island, Kefalonia does not have a reputation for nightlife in the same way that other Greek Islands do, and thankfully so. However, holidaymakers and visitors can still find some really great clubs and bars in some towns and resorts if they want and if you want to party the night away it is possible to do so on Kefalonia. You just need to know where to look.

The capital city of Argostoli is the main place for nightlife. There are a number of great nightclubs and music bars on the main street and on a cool evening it is a real pleasure to roam from tavern to tavern stopping along the way to browse in the night market or to have a bite to eat. Move through the old town and the old squares and head down to the harbour and the waterfront where you'll find a number of great tavernas to watch the sunset from.

There are also a number of popular clubs and bars in all of the main resorts like Skala, Sami, Poros, Lixouri and Fiscardo. In addition you will nearly always find parties going down on the beaches of the resorts during the summer months.

Kefalonia is without any shadow of doubt the ideal island for a quiet holiday by the sea, enjoying its golden beaches and crystal clear waters. Nature is the undisputed queen with its multifaceted landscapes from the lush greenery, to the highest mountains and unique wildlife.

So it is not known for its nightlife, but there are some bars and clubs for those who want to have fun at night, without great expectations and always having not in mind Mykonos nightlife.

Sometimes, especially during the high season, there are some theme parties are organized on the most famous beaches of the island.

Most of the nightlife is concentrated in Argostoli, the capital, with modern clubs and big discos to have fun all night with dance music and cocktails. Also in other places of the island (Sami, Skala, Fiscardo, Lixouri and Poros) there are bars and disco clubs to spend long nights.

Discos and Nightclubs in Kefalonia
Among the major clubs and discos of Kefalonia, the best place is the undisputed Bass Club. It's the most exciting and vibrant club in

Kefalonia. Located in Argostoli (near the main square), it offers a true experience of nightlife. Traditional non-stop dance-music, both Greek and foreign, with guests, DJs and live music, in order to ensure that everyone has fun all night, all year round. The entertainment program increases the adrenaline and allows visitors to enjoy a real "dance overdose." Recently renovated and more luxurious than ever the Bass Club adds color to the after hours in Kefalonia and provides an overview of how people enjoy in Greece.

Another famous nightclub in the center of Argostoli, is the Cinema Music Club, and as the name suggests it is obtained by the renovation of an old cinema, keeping the same seats and an old projector. The dance floor is large enough, and the club plays the usual music dance, house, hip-hop, remix, etc.. As one of the few nightclubs of Kefalonia, the Cinema Club has a nice atmosphere and anyone who wants to enjoy the evening and night until late must come here!

North of the island, in the picturesque village of Fiskardo, there is a famous nightclub open every night during the summer, since 1995: the Kastro Club. It's a great club that once was an old mine, located in a cool area and surrounded by greenery, at just 500 meters from the port of Fiscardo.

Built in stone on four levels following an amphitheater shape around the large central dance floor, the club covers an area of 700 square meters. with tables and chairs arranged under the palm trees. The musical program for summer fun includes a wide variety of genres, such as rock n 'roll, soul, pop, new wave, reggae, hip hop and greek hits. Do not miss the theme parties, organized every year and attracting many visitors: the "bras de fer" party, the party of the tropical night and Greek night are just a few memorable ones! The club or part of it is of course open to bookings for private parties with friends, to celebrate birthdays and other festive occasions.

Bars in Kefalonia
In addition to nightclubs and discos, Kefalonia and in particular its capital Argostoli, is dotted with modern cafes and bars, where entertaining for a drink before going to the disco. We suggest the Stavento Bar, on the beach front of Argostoli, with spectacular sea views, especially at sunset, populated by locals and tourists, which is a place to relax day and night.

Just outside Argostoli, on the main road to Lassi, the So Simple is a lively bar suitable for all ages. You enter through an arch decorated with palms and exotic flowers, part outdoors, part indoors, the bar offers a tranquil setting offering seats to about 100 people.

The music is played both by two huge plasma screens placed on the wall and tuned on Sky, and by a DJ who plays everything from classic 70s, to metal, rock, blues, reggae, hip-hop and rap. However, the music is not too loud to prevent the conversation, and is ideal to spend a pleasant and relaxing evening at reasonable prices and with excellent service.

On the southern tip of the island, just on the beach of Skala, we find one of the best bars of Kefalonia: the Capitain's Bar.

Open since 1987, the bar is renowned for its excellent service and warm atmosphere. Here you can relax in the evening sipping a refreshing cocktail or beers, staring at the sea, listening to music while chatting with friends - it is the ideal place to meet new people.

Recently, the owners of the Capitain's Bar opened in front of it the new Capitain's Lounge. It is a new, exclusive lounge bar where you can celebrate in style your special occasions (birthdays, anniversaries).

For a more unusual experience, you have to try the Zebra Bar in Skala. The bar is very nice and decorated with wooden furniture and bright lights. Here you can enjoy live music upstairs and have a party downstairs with a wild zebra dancing around (of course the zebra is someone in costume).

Still to the south, on the beach of Poros, a very popular place is the Zanza Bar. The bar is famous for its excellent service and friendly atmosphere. It offers a wide selection of cocktails (more than 45), among the best on the island. If you are looking for a place to relax, enjoy listening to good music, or try a couple of "brand-new" cocktails, the Zanza Bar is the perfect place!

Kefalonia' Resort Guide

Resort Guide to Lourdas Kefalonia

Another Kefalonia resort for those holidaymakers seeking out a more peaceful and tranquil holiday is the resort of Lourdas. Spend a couple of weeks in Lourdas and you really will forget all of the worries you left behind back in the UK and you'll never want to go back. Ideal for those who truly want to get away from it all, with self-catering villas dotted around the small village, Lourdas offers all of the essentials of a quiet Greek break, from the perfect beach to the prefect scenery and surroundings, without any of the irritations brash resorts, loud partygoers and throngs of people. It has begun to see a little bit of development, although not yet noticeably so, and there are now one or two hotels popping up, although they are very small and tucked away in quiet lanes. The village has been around for hundreds of years, but feels very modern thanks to all the buildings being rebuilt post-earthquake. It is worth checking out where your chosen accommodation will be situated though many apartments and villas are by the sea, whilst others are in the village itself, which is on a steep hill. For those who want a lazy holiday or who are less able to negotiate hills, it is important to book wisely.

That said however, many visitors to Lourdas, as with Svoronata, will choose to hire a car for the duration of their holiday, as there are plenty of other sights to see around the island and the main towns of Argostoli and Lassi are very close by and easy to reach by car. If you want to get out and about and see a little of the Island's history, apart from visiting the various museums and sights in Argostoli, you could also head to the Monastery of Sissia. Rumor has it that the monastery was founded in the 13th century by St Francis of Assisi and it was once an incredibly wealthy monastery famed for its intellectual and talented monks, such as the painters Gerasimos Kokkinos and Tsangorola. The current incarnation was rebuilt when the old monastery was destroyed in the earthquake. Follow the road out of town to drive around the beautiful beaches and coves nearby as well as to explore the slopes of the awe-inspiring Mount Einos and the spectacular views to the sea below.

Really though, a holiday in Lourdas is all about finding a little slice of Mediterranean paradise and doing very little for a couple of weeks. The village is simple to negotiate and well designed as it was rebuilt after the earthquake there are some wonderful small squares and the main square has a spring and a giant plane tree that offers shade to a charming café for the locals. Amble into the square in the morning for a coffee and quiet read of your book or a chat with one of the local characters. If you are feeling energetic, take a stroll into the lush countryside around the village walk amongst the cypress and olive trees, the elegant palm trees and the endless vegetable gardens set between houses and tavernas. Have a quiet drink in the evening (there are no noisy drinks in Lourdas) and then fall asleep to that most wonderful of nighttime sounds utter silence.

Resort Guide to Argostoli Kefalonia

Argostoli is the beating heart of Kefalonia, a town that has managed to embrace modern life whilst holding on to its centuries old traditional character. Argostli has been the island's capital since 1757 and is also capital of the whole Ithaca prefecture. The town is laid out in the traditional Greek way, designed amphitheatrically so that it looks out over the stunning Koustavos lagoon, a lagoon that glistens blue-green every morning and is often packed with everything from tiny fishing boats to vast private yachts. The town has an abundance of wonderful architecture worth exploring, from expansive and bustling town squares to charming picture postcard churches and endless rows of neoclassical buildings, (although most of the original architecture was destroyed first by German bombs and then by the earthquake in 1953). Argostoli is also surrounded on all sides by lush green forests covering imposing mountains and is connected to the rest of the island by the large Drapano stone bridge that crosses the lagoon.

For tourists and visitors this combination of the old Argostoli remains and the new layout of the town in wide, spacious streets and squares lined with gorgeous thick palm trees and dotted with benches (all filled with old, lively and characterful locals) makes for a charming place to visit. Additionally, Argostoli is a working port that supports not just the occasional cruise liner, but also local sightseeing tours, small ferries and fishing boats that go out early every morning and then sell their fish on the seafront. Indeed, take a stroll by the sea early in the morning and you will get to witness the wonderful melodic bartering going on between the local hoteliers and tavern owners and the fish sellers at the fish market.

This is the joy of Argostoli, a hive of traditional local businesses and local traditions, mixed with the constant throng of tourists enjoying the local attractions and sights.

If you do fancy a day or two of sightseeing, Argostoli has plenty to offer. Up on Roku Vergoti street there is the fascinating Museum of Archaeology containing a wonderful collection of excavated Mycenaean relics that were found all over Kefalonia. Next to that is the Historical and Cultural Museum that displays the various relics left by the many occupiers of Kefalonia (including the British) and their tools, weapons, furniture and traditional dress. Other attractions include the Napier Garden, the Korgialenios Library and the monuments to revolutionaries on Rizospaston Street. For fine views head up to the Kampanas Square and the renovated belfry tower that offers the best spot to take in the lagoon and the town below. A bit further out there are places such as Farao Hill, also offering fine views of the town and the magical Katavothres caves found near to the Aghioi Theodoroi lighthouse. The lighthouse itself sits at the edge of the Lassi Peninsula and offers visitors some spectacular sunsets. All of this can be reached via the Giro of Lassi, a winding road that leads from Argostoli to Lassi.

For shopping, head to the retail district on Lithostroto street, a long and busy street offering every kind of tradesman, artisan and local produce as well as numerous bakeries, eateries, gift shops, clothes shops, boutiques, hairdressers, supermarkets and book shops. There are all the usual necessities such as banks and buses, taxis and car hire and down in the harbor you can get ferries to nearby Lixouri every half hour and which take around twenty minutes journey time.

The best bit about Argostoli though are the balmy early evenings when you can stroll from tavern to restaurant to tavern before browsing the late markets and engaging with the local traders. Whether you wander around the bustling Valianos Square or the coastal public market, or whether you head to the Saturday market before dining at one of the well-known restaurants nearby the Anonymos, Kalafatis and Diana Taverna all have great reputations make sure you do it with a glass of the local Robolo wine in your hand.

Resort Guide to Lassi Kefalonia

Lassi is Kefalonia's oldest and most established resort town and an ideal place to base yourself to explore the rest of the island. This fantstic resort is only three kilometers away from the capital of the island, Argostoli and has been attracting visitors for more than twenty years thanks to its spectacular views out over the Lixouri peninsular. Nowadays that peninsular has been developed considerably more than other parts of the island so if you are looking for a tranquil and mellow Kefalonia resort you might want to think about looking elsewhere. If however you are looking for all the usual elements of a traditional Greek holiday great beaches, crystal blue sea, water parks and watersports, endless bars, tavernas as well as a wide range of eateries then Lassi is ideal.

Only minutes away from the airport, Lassi is perfect if you want to jump on a plane and be out on your sunbed a few hours later. There's no denying Lassi can get very busy in high season but this is because the resort is home to one of the finest sandy beaches in Kefalonia and a selection of large and modern hotels that look out over the peninsular. Most of these hotels (such as the Plati Yialos and Makris Yialos or The White Rocks) are only minutes from the soft white sand and afford visitors the pleasure of sunset walks barefoot along the waters edge, taking in the incredible scenery (photographers will find those sunsets irresistible) and stopping off at any of the small tavernas or traditional local restaurants that take your fancy. In addition to the main beach there are a couple of other long beaches offering all the usual watersports and holiday activities as well as some quiet and peaceful coves if you want to get away from the crowds and noise. With a number of popular mini-markets and handicraft fairs as well as traditional local shops, Lassi is a resort that has everything you will need and will perfectly suit those of you looking for a relaxing family holiday.

When deciding on Lassi it is worth checking on the location of your hotel as the resort is filled with accommodation, some of it close to the sea and some of it further back tucked away in cool shaded streets behind old palm trees or higher up in the hills. If you are looking for a lazy holiday or are not particularly disposed to enjoying walking up steep roads then you'll want to make sure your hotel is not in the hills!

Lassi does offer other the opportunity to see some of the local sights too. Its proximity to Argostoli make sit the perfect base from which to hire a car and see the rest of the island and on the outskirts of the resort there are a wide range of pristine and empty sandy beaches that are easily reachable by car.

It also has a number of local attractions within the resort itself, such as the cave of St Gerasimos (St Gerasimos is the patron saint of Kefalonia). The cave is where Gerasimos lived for five years when he first arrived on the island and there is now a charming old church next to the cave dedicated to him, the Church of Odos Spiliou Agios Gerasimou. For budding photographers this is a great spot to get some wonderful pictures, not just of the local landscape, but also of the wonderful caves and church. The insides of the church are elegant and ornate, filled with gentle paintings and icons and well worth spending time visiting.

Lassi may be the main resort on Kefalonia, but it has managed to do this whilst retaining some of its traditional charm and remaining relatively low-key, in spite of all the recent development. Choose the right hotel and you will find yourself and your family coming back again and again.

Resort Guide to Fiscardo Kefalonia

Much loved by yacht owners, artists, celebrities, well-heeled visitors from Italy and holidaymakers alike, Fiscardo is one of Kefalonia's most charming and elegant destinations. It is the northernmost town on the island and is a port (and fishing town) that offers ferry routes out to Ithaca ports of Lefkada and Frikes. It is beloved by artists for its Venetian buildings painted in pastel colors and the historic tavernas that look out over the water, not to mention the charms of the local fisherman who remain there despite the rising prices brought on by the influx of wealthy visitors. Fiscardo managed to avoid the brunt of the destruction brought on by the 1953 earthquake in comparison with other towns and villages and consequently retains a great deal of original Venetian architecture which is why it is so popular in summer (sometimes a little too popular!) Many people choose to visit rather than stay in Fiscardo (as the hotels there are very expensive), and there are some fantastic restaurants and tavernas along the waterfront, with The Captain's Cabin and Faros often described as the best restaurants on the island. Even a coffee in a waterfront café is a delight sitting in the sun watching the fishermen get their nets ready for their next trip out to sea.

Fiscardo is packed with things to see and do. A lot of people head to Fiscardo for the shopping alone, with seemingly endless backstreets of tiny gift shops, craft shops, tavernas and cafes round every corner. The streets are gorgeous to walk around and simply window-shop as they are lined both sides with the traditional Kefalonian 18th century buildings, balconies, tiled roofs and grapevines. The harbor walk is a must-see too and if you follow the headland around from the harbor you will eventually come to a small but delightful beach. For those people after a bit of history there are a couple of old buildings to explore. Follow steps from the harbor up to the Panagia of Platiteras Church and Monastery and explore a wonderful area that was left untouched by the 1953 earthquake. Additionally you can spend some time admiring the ruins of an ancient Byzantine church and its remaining Venetian architecture. Another trip worth making is over to the Lighthouse of Cape Fiscardo. This gorgeous old lighthouse was built in 1892 and stands proudly on a sliver of land that juts out into the sea. Lastly, check out the harbor museum that has a fascinating display depicting how the village has changed over the last few years.

If you want to head out and about then there are some stunning spots near to Fiscardo as the west coast of Kefalonia is well known for having the most impressive beaches and landscape. Heading south from Fiscardo (probably in a hire car) you'll get to Assos village which features one of Greece's most picturesque ports as well as a stunning Venetian fortress and row upon row of pastel painted Venetian buildings. Further on you'll get to Myrtos beach, the most spectacular beach in all of Greece and consistently voted into the top ten of best beaches in the world thanks to its white sand, turquoise sea and surrounding tall cliffs. Further still you'll discover a seemingly endless choice of untouched and picturesque beaches and coves, most of which you can have all to yourself.

Finally, while in Fiscardo it is worth taking the opportunity to hire a boat or go out on a boat tour for the day as the stretch of water between Fiscardo and Ithaca is something you will never forget. A tour is preferable as they will be able to guide you around all the hidden sea coves and caves, point out all the marine life, from octopi to the resident monachus monachus to all the usual Mediterranean fish (at least the ones that haven't been wiped out by overfishing!)

Resort Guide to Assos Kefalonia

If you were to conjure up a picture of the archetypal sleepy Mediterranean Greek village featuring untouched villages and houses that have seen little change over the last couple of centuries then you might well picture Assos. Assos is the ideal destination for those holidaymakers who really want to get away from it all. With that in mind it is worth pointing out that like a couple of other resorts, car hire is an absolute must if you are going to stay in Assos. However, if you do choose to do that and to hire a car, you will be rewarded with perhaps the most charming, relaxing and welcoming village in the whole of Kefalonia, if not all of the Greek Islands.

The impression of Assos as an untouched Greek village starts on the approach road into the village. An exhilarating ride of endless hairpin bends and fantastic views leads you from the road along the cliff top to the delightful and romantic village of Assos waiting for you at the bottom. From the moment you enter Assos you get the sense of a place that is lost in time, from the small square at its center with the local restaurants and tavernas to the multi-colored fishing boats of all shapes and sizes bobbing up and down in the harbor (and the odd luxury yacht too). As with most places the bulk of the original architecture was damaged by war and earthquake, but in Assos most of the Venetian architecture can still be seen in ruins dotted around the village which only adds to the timeless feel of the place, sitting as it does amongst the gorgeous colored houses nestled into the hillsides and around the bay. This secluded village is the very definition of romantic, from the horse-shoe shaped harbor to the surrounding dramatic coastline with its waves crashing onto white rocks and hills covered from head to toe in lush forests of pine and cypress all topped off with the ruins of an old Venetian fortress sitting on high above the peninsula. That old fortress, Assos Castle, was originally built in 1584 and represented one of the largest and most imposing landmarks on the whole island. Nowadays there are enough remains to get a good idea of the original scale of the castle, and they also offer spectacular views from an incredibly beautiful spot. The trip is best made early in the morning or in the cooler part of the afternoon as it is a long and winding track to get there.

Other sights worth seeing include the assorted beautiful Venetian ruins (but be careful, some are in a very poor state) and the various churches located nearby. These include the Church of the Virgin Mary that sits approximately half way up the fortress road (and which provides a fantastic resting place en route to stop and take in the views of the harbor and countryside); the Church of Asios Giorgios, painted in a light pink color and built in 1871, only a few hundred yards from the village square and the Madonna of the Sand, which sits right on the beach. Additionally you will no doubt spend countless hours ambling around the village itself and taking in the locals themselves, many of who will stop and chat, as well as sights along the waterfront such as the old cannon and the war memorial.

However Assos is really the perfect resort for those who want to get off the beaten track and indulge their passion for hiking and biking, photography and bird-watching, and generally just slowing down for a couple of weeks in beautiful, natural surroundings. The smell of the fields and herbs, flowers and olive groves all around you, combined with the constant crashing of waves against the cliffs, will soothe your soul and reinvigorate your life. And should you want to get away for a day and stock up on supplies or just have an evening out, then the capital city of Aggostoli is only about 4o minutes away in the car. Chances are, however, that you will find all you need in the small shops, small restaurants, charming beaches and clear waters of this charming Kefalonia village and harbor.

Resort Guide to Skala Kefalonia

Skala is Kefalonia's most popular resort and one that has developed from a small fishing village to a modern and fun resort in just twenty years. Yet it has done so without ruining what made it inviting in the first place and has thankfully not gone down the 'loud and brash' route of many other Greek Island resorts. However, that's not to say it doesn't offer all the usual Greek Holiday resort conveniences and attractions. Skala is a proper resort destination now and offers everything you would expect from lively bars and the occasional nightclub through to miles and miles of fantastic blue flagged beaches of both sand and shingle, all surrounded by gorgeous sweet smelling and impossibly high pine trees.

When it comes to fun and attractions Skala has something for everyone. On the beach you'll find a choice of activities ranging from extreme sports jet skiing, paragliding etc through to relaxations aimed at the more horizontally inclined sun loungers, umbrellas and drinks with umbrellas, all served up on your own little corner of the beach. Skala may be popular but it is quiet enough that you can get a spot on the beach all to yourself and not worry about barging shoulders with people lying next to you.

In the resort itself there is everything you need, mostly on the main street, from supermarkets and gift shops, cash points, banks and pharmacies to bakeries, local food and craft markets to a wide array of different tavernas and bars (from small and friendly local tavernas to larger tourist bars with music and dancing). Additionally, if you fancy a gentle stroll around a quieter area then you can head over to the original fishing village which is a charming and friendly place to visit. You can lose hours wandering around the maze of narrow cobblestoned streets amongst the houses, cafes, tavernas (with locals sat outside playing cards) and fishing huts. Though still picturesque the modern village was rebuilt in 1956 after the earthquake destroyed almost all of the original village.

If you fancy a break from the resort it is worth exploring some of the history dotted around Skala. For example you can find a 3rd century ancient Roman villa on the edge of the village which is free to visit and definitely worth seeing, if only for the stunning well-preserved mosaics. Similarly if you head a couple of miles out of town you'll find the remains of the Temple of Apollo which archaeologists have dated back to 600 BC. Lastly, up in the hills there are numerous ruins for the original Skala village. For many years it was possible to stroll around these remains and ruins and picture what life used to be like and thought this is still possible a few of the sites have since been bought by developers and new villas are starting to spring up. Nevertheless it is worth going there if only to see the old churches, houses and olive presses and the wild goats and other wildlife living there.

Another escape from the beach resort, should you decide you need one, is to head out into the fields and hills around Skala where you can wander amongst the goats and sheep running free and the thousands of local beehives which are used to make an amazing Kefalonian thyme flavored honey. There are numerous trails that wind through the valleys and hills and between smallholdings and vineyards, olive and orange groves and endless rows of fig trees, walnut trees and almond trees.

Finally there is Potamaki beach, just down the coast, which is recently been declared a conservation area thanks to the extremely rare loggerhead turtles laying their eggs there. Take the opportunity to go on one of the turtle watches at night it is something you will never forget.

Resort Guide to Lixouri Kefalonia

Lixouri is often referred to as the second city of Kefalonia and is the second largest town in terms of population size after Argostoli, with approximately 3000 inhabitants living there. Many people prefer it to Argostoli because it offers most of the same facilities and services but is just that little bit quieter. It is the Paliki Peninsula capital town and has gained a reputation as being one of the friendliest and most interesting places on the island. Other villages and resorts boast better beaches and more attractive buildings, but Lixouri is famous for the charm of the locals that live there and the entertainment they provide. That's not to say the area is not attractive. Though not blessed with the awesome cliffs, lush valleys and spectacular beaches of other parts of the island the Paliki Peninsula is elegantly beautiful in its own way, offering a flatter, gentler landscape packed with farmland, olive groves, vineyards on gentle hills and long stretches of fruit groves.

What Lixouri does offer is a wealth of attractions that are worth visiting whether you are staying there or in another resort. This does mean it can get very busy, particularly around the harbor area and waterfront in the height of summer, as lots of people arrive from and depart for Argostoli via the ferries that leave every twenty minutes. You'll also see a lot of people stopping to admire all the statues placed around the town, each depicting famous figures from the island's history, from freedom fighter Georgios Typaldos Iavokatos to the Bishop of Kerkini Illias Miniatis and local benefactor Kalavrita Stamos Petritis. The most famous bronze of all is that of Andreas Laskaratos the island's most famous satirical poet. His statue was strategically placed out on the town quay with his back purposely turned towards Argostoli to represent the long running feud between the towns that dates back to 1757 when the capital was moved by the Venetians to Argostoli. That was not something went down well with the good people of Lixouri and they have held a grudge ever since. Another historical must-see is the resored mansion building of Typaldos-Iakovatos, one of the only Venetian buildings in the town to survive the earthquake. Restored in the 1980's by the Greek Ministry of Culture the building now houses the Lixouri Public Library and the excellent Typaldos-Iakovatos Museum and is decorated inside with intricate wood panel ceilings and frescoes and contains a fantastic collection of ancient manuscript gospels, icons and furniture.

For those who want to get out and about around Lixouri car hire is a must. Hiring your own car allows you to head out and see some of the fantastic beaches nearby, often deserted and all beautiful. Particular highlights include the beaches at Xi, Lepedes, Petani and Mega Lakkos all of which are great for swimming, and are uncrowded and sandy. Additionally you can drive between Lixouri and Argostoli along one of the most scenic routes on the island, following a flat road until Livadi where you climb upwards on an exhilarating cliff road with wonderful panoramic views across the island. If you get time it is also worth visiting the Katavothres pits where thousands of gallons of sea-water disappear into the earth (only to resurface at the Melissani Lakes.)

Whether you're staying there (and it is a great place to stay) or just visiting, make some time for Lixouri, if only to take the ferry between there and Argostoli. A tour of the local attractions followed by dinner along Lixouri waterfront and then a night ferry back under a wide bright moon (with the town lights shimmering on shore) is the quintessential Kefalonia experience. Make sure you try it.

Resort Guide to Katelios Kefalonia

Katelios is a Kefalonia resort that seems to inspire fierce loyalty in everyone who stays there, so much so that people tend to come back year after year to the same place. Perhaps that has something to do with the combination of laid back atmosphere and dramatic scenery (as well as stunning beaches) that gives the resort everything you could possibly ask for when heading to a Greek

Island for a holiday. Katelios is located down in the south-eastern part of Kefalonia and sits on an extensive flat plain between the villages of Ratzakli, Markopoulo, Mavrata and Hionata. It has fabulous views out over the glistening blue sea towards Zante, the neighboring island and also across the Greek mainland and is surrounded by beautiful farmland and some impressive rolling rocky hills. For the last hundred years the village was made up of just a few fishing cottages (some of which are still there) but over the last decade it has gradually been turned into a charming little resort and holiday destination, thanks mainly to its beautiful beaches.

Katelios is split between the old village of Anos Ketelios and Kato Katelios, the more modern resort area. This makes for the perfect mix of old and new, with everything you need from a quiet holiday resort on the one hand, plus enough history and beautiful old buildings and remains on the other. Consequently if you want an afternoon or two of culture and history it is possible to get lost in the local area from the old church bell tower remains to a number of old ruins left over from the earthquake and from Katelios' ancient role as a trading port during the Venetian period. These include the ruins of an ancient pier and the old mole in the bay. Additionally there is evidence that there was a Roman settlement on Katelios and the remains, sitting just off Aghia beach (the main beach in Katelios) are worth a visit too.

For those looking for a bit of nature and wildlife Katelios also has a lot to offer. It is one of the best spots on the whole island for nature walks, with a number of trails on the outskirts of the village. There are a number of hideaways tucked into the hills as the resort is popular with birdwatchers and best of all it is a great place to see Loggerhead Turtles. Indeed there is a local NGO, called the Katelios Group which is dedicated to protecting the turtles and which offers educational tours of their habitats.

However, if nature and history are not your bag and all you want is sun, sea and the occasional evening in the local taverna then Katelios offers that too. There are a small number of tavernas in the center of the village and enough shops and bars to keep you well stocked for a week or two. The whole atmosphere is very easy going and less commercial than other resorts. The restaurants in the village serve beautiful, simple food, (mostly Mezedes and meat of course) and the bars and restaurants on the waterfront offer the perfect setting for an evening meal.

Resort Guide to Svoronata Kefalonia

If you're looking for an idyllic resort holiday without all the sound and fury and without the usual throng of your fellow tourists from the UK then you might want to consider spending your holidays in the Svoronata resort area. Despite its proximity to the capital city of Argostoli and Kefalonia International Airport Svoronata is one of the most peaceful holiday resorts that you will ever have the pleasure of staying in, more akin to a sleepy town than a full blown resort. Svoronata itself is a traditional low-key Greek village that is compact, flat and easy to get around. But it is also located amidst some of the most gorgeous Mediterranean scenery imaginable, making it the perfect archetypal Greek holiday spot.

Situated in the south-west area of Kefalonia, in the Livathos region, Svoronata is easy to get to thanks to being right next to the airport (don't worry flights arrive so infrequently that you will barely notice the airport) and is ideal for older groups, wheelchair users, families or people who want quiet, lazy holidays. There are no hills and no noise, no drunken tourists (or very few anyway) and there is a genuine sense of stillness and contentment in the town, thanks to the elegant beauty of that surrounding scenery. From lush olive groves and orange groves to miles and miles of fruit orchards and fields bursting with flowers in the summer, Svoronata is exceptionally beautiful. Like most of the resorts on Kefalonia it also has a stunning selection of sandy beaches nearby although you need to remember that the village itself is about a mile inland. If you want to walk to the nearby beaches of Ammes Avithos or Ai Helis then it will probably take you about half an hour (depending on how hot it is) but you would be better jumping in a car for a couple of minutes. Indeed staying in Svoronata is probably only advisable if you hire a car for the duration of your holiday. Whilst the village is stunning and offers beautiful accommodation, from small to large hotels, apartments to villas all with their own pools and all spread all over the village, there is very little to do in the way of shopping or sightseeing, nightlife or other activities. A car puts all of that within easy reach in nearby Argostoli or Lassi. What's more, staying in Svoronata with a hire car opens up the whole of Kefalonia to you, thanks to the central location of the village on the island and the fact that it is easy to access any of the other resorts from there.

Driving out from Svoronata also allows you to see parts of Kefalonia that many visitors don't get to see, as one sleepy village or hamlet rolls into another, following the olive-lined windy roads and the ruins of old houses hit by the various wars and earthquakes that have tormented the island. You'll have to get a map however Kefalonia isn't big on organized roads or even street names but that's half the fun and you'll find no shortage of locals sitting on benches by the side of the road ready to offer directions (that may or may not get you to your intended destination!)

However, chances are that despite the lure of the road, you'll spend most of your holiday in Svoronata itself. From the wonderfully charming locals sat on their doorsteps who you will meet every day, to ambling gently in the afternoon sun through the endless village gardens packed with colorful and scented flowers and fruit trees, to days spent peacefully dozing on the quiet beaches, Svoronata will provide you with the perfect antidote to modern life. There are a couple of things to see nearby the Svoronata church is one of the biggest on the island (and is decorated with some incredible frescoes) and there is a windmill down a nondescript village lane where Lord Byron spent many a day composing his odes. There are a couple of small mini-marts for basic goods and a couple of tavernas for eating out. But in reality you'll be in Svoronata for the tranquility it offers and if you wanted to, you could spend a week or two here without seeing another soul and it would be bliss.

Car Hire in Kefalonia

Kefalonia is considered to be the least affected Greek island by tourism. Though Kefalonia plays host to thousands of tourists each year, the bus service is limited and the island is extremely hilly after all it is named after the Greek word "head".

Renting a car in Kefalonia is not only a wise choice, it is an economical one. Kefalonia has both local and international car hire outlets within local towns and at the airport that can also be arranged online so hiring a car could never be easier.

It is recommended that you compare prices as they can vary however for simplicity and a stress free holiday Kefalonia.co.uk recommends that you buy online prior to flying to Kefalonia. Car-Hire-Kefalonia.com is perfect for hiring a car in Kefalonia. All cars are come with air conditioning, free delivery and pickup and 24 hour road side assistance should you require it.

Caution: Kefalonia is a hilly island with narrow roads that travel up to the higest villages. If you are intending to explore please be careful, many of the hillside roads have no barriers! Take your time, drive carefully and enjoy your holiday!

The Language

Greek is the main language of Kefalonia and the Ionian Islands. It is a beautiful language but a difficult one for English speakers to master by virtue of it having a completely different alphabet on top of the normal problems that come with learning languages. Additionally the grammar of the Greek language is even more complicated. The nouns are split into 3 genders each of them with their own different case endings in both singular and plural and each requiring adjectives and articles to match the case, number and gender.

Thankfully however you will not need to know Greek when you visit Kefalonia as nearly everyone will speak English. The tourism industry is the number one industry in Kefalonia and it is growing ever more popular as a holiday destination with Italians, French, Germans and the English, as well as the Greeks themselves. Because so many of the locals work in tourism and work in the resorts, English is essentially their second language and is spoken everywhere. (Because of the island's close ties with Italy most locals also speak Italian too.)

That being said it is worth learning some important phrases and taking a phrasebook with you when you go. Firstly, it makes a good impression with the locals if you are at least trying to make an effort and speak their language and secondly if you do head out from the resorts and end up touring some of the little villages you will encounter older locals who do not speak English. In such cases you might want to have a phrasebook on hand in case you need to ask directions or get some help.

Money and Banks

At the time of writing the currency in Greece remains the Euro, despite all the problems the country and the economy have been going through. You can find the latest exchange rates on the internet and should shop around when looking to get currency for your holiday. Euros are issued in denominations of 5, 10, 20, 50, 100, 200 and 500 notes. Coins come in denominations of 1, 2, 5, 10, 20, and 50 cents as well as 1 and 2 Euro coins.

The Greek word for Bank is (tra-peza) and you will see it on a sign outside of any bank. In Greece, and Kefalonia, banks open between 8am and 2pm Mondays through Thursdays and from 8am until 1:30pm on Fridays. Generally banks close over the weekend and on bank holidays, religious holidays and festivals. All will accept Visa, Mastercard and American Express and UK debit cards carrying the Maestro or Cirrus symbol will also be accepted in most places. There are a number of different banks in Poros, Lixouri, Fiskardo and Argostoli. You can also find atm machines in all of those places plus Sami and Skala.

Local Industry

Kefalonia is a small and ancient island that has a number of traditional industries that have been going for hundreds of years. Most of them have struggled in recent years however and tourism has become the dominant industry on the island in the last couple of decades. Nevertheless, local industries do survive.

Fishing was once the largest industry on the island thanks to the local waters being packed with fish. Alas, over-fishing has led to a massive drop in the number of available fish around Kefalonia (and other Greek islands) and though there is still a small local fishing industry it is smaller than in its heyday. Nowadays the harbors of Lixouri and Argostoli are the important fishing centers and it is worth heading down to their harbors early in the morning to watch the local fishermen and taverna owners haggling and trading fish. Additionally there are a number of large fish farms floating on the outskirts of Argostoli and Lixouri.

Over the last twenty years wine making has grown into one of the larger industries on the island. There has been a tradition of wine making on Keflaonia for hundreds and even thousands of years, with Homer having referenced the Kefalonian wines, but it is only in the last twenty years that local producers have finessed their wine to make it more palatable to western style tastes. This was started by Nicholas Cosmetatos, who set up the Gentilini label and who fused classical Kefalonian wine flavors with a new method of making wine. He was soon followed by the Metaxas label and three or four other local producers. Nowadays Kefalonia has three appellations – Mavrodaphne, Muscat and Robola.

Another major part of the Kefalonia economy is the production of olive oil. Up until the late 18th century Kefalonia simply produced enough olive oil for the people who lived on the island. This soon changed when their Venetian conquerors urgently required more olive plantations after losing Crete and the Peloponnese. Consequently the island started exporting olive oil to Venice. Up until 1953 Kefalonia had somewhere in excess of two hundred different oil presses producing oil. After the earthquake however there remained only thirteen. Kefalonia has more than a million olive trees that cover more than fifty per cent of the island. These thirteen presses are crucial to the island's rural and local economy, producing two main varieties of olive oil, 'theiako oil' and 'koroneiki oil'. There are a couple of other smaller varieties known as 'matolia' and 'ntopia.'

Finally of course there is tourism, the main industry now on Kefalonia. Thanks in part to its stunning beauty and also in recent years thanks to that movie, people come to Kefalonia from all over Europe and the wider world. As a holiday destination it is extremely popular with Italians, but also Greeks themselves, Germans, French and the English. Most people stay in the resort of Lassi or else in Skala or Katelios. Consequently English is virtually a second language and Italian is very common too.

The most surprising thing about Kefalonia is that a large percentage of the locals leave the island at the end of the season and don't return during the winter period. The island is so dependent on tourism that there is very little work available at the end of the tourism season and it is therefore not possible for most of the locals to make a living there.

Healthcare in Kefalonia

The most common ailments for travellers to Kefalonia are the same ones that travellers get the world over – stomach upsets. The change of diet to food that uses a lot more oils and serves up endless oily foods inevitably leads to some rumblings down below. But give it a couple of days and most people adjust. It helps to add lemon to the oil to dilute all that oil and you should try to drink plenty of water too. However it is probably best to drink bottled water whilst on the island, as it is available everywhere at little cost and is a necessary precaution. Try to avoid any meat dishes that look like they were left over from lunch. As mentioned in the food section a lot of restaurants will do most of their cooking at lunch and then leave stuff to cool or reheat it in the evenings. If you've got a delicate belly you might want to order something fresh to be grilled in the evenings.

The beaches are relatively safe – the main dangers are the occasional jellyfish or sea urchin. If you do encounter a sea urchin make sure you get all the spikes out.

Should you need to get a doctor (or dentist) the best place to head to is the chemists (farmakion.) They will be able to point you to an English-speaking doctor. Similarly they can handle prescription drugs if you lose yours, or all of the minor complaints such as stomach bugs, headaches and mosquito bites.

When it comes to more serious illnesses or injuries if you come from inside Europe you will be covered by the EHIC (European health Insurance Card) which will entitle you to receive medical treatment when in another European country either for free or at a significantly reduced rate. In addition, people of all nationalities are covered in Greece when it comes to emergency treatment in a public hospital. If you find yourself in an emergency simply dial 166.

Public hospitals are a mixed bag in Greece – everyone is very well trained and will offer you nothing but the best health care, but they are seriously under-funded and as a consequence their health care system is considered to be one of the worst in all of Europe. Relatives are required to bring in bed linen and food for patients and it is a good idea to have private health care via a good insurance policy if you can afford it. That said, the two main hospitals in Kefalonia are better than most in Greece; there is one in Lixouri and a larger main hospital in Argostoli. Both are excellent.

Loggerhead Turtles in Kefalonia

Although Zante is the most important nesting site for these turtles which are an endangered species, there is a nesting site at Kefalonia called Kaminia beach. The sea Turtle Protection Society work hard and long to protect the fascinating creatures when they come in to nest on the beach.

The females heave and tug themselves across the beach to find a nesting site digging holes and laying small round eggs. An average nest would have 120 eggs and once they are safely covered with warm sand the female returns to the water. Some females will lay as many as four times during the nesting season and the eggs take about two months to hatch.

The baby turtles dig their way out at night and head instinctively for the sea. This natural pattern can be disrupted by noise and lights. Sometimes the body clock in the baby turtles goes away and they pop out during the day. If you see a turtle its best not to touch it as its essential to their survival that they make their own way to the sea. After leaving the beach in the day.

The Marine Turtle Project was set up some years ago to observe and record the nesting female turtles on the beaches near to the villages of Skala and Ratzakli on the south-eastern tip of the island. This project has continued to this day and incorporated a conservation programme to promote the protection of the beaches where these creatures lay their eggs.

Just outside Katelios you will find a little old schoolhouse which has been transformed and is now the base for The Katelios Group for the Research and Protection of Marine and Terrestrial Life. The group was founded in 1994 and consists mainly of local people with an interest in the long term future of Kefalonia. Volunteer students from all over the world stay on a camp site close by whilst collecting data and making their observations on marine life. The group are also involved with setting up self sufficient commercially viable projects that fall under the heading of Environmentally Sustainable Community development.

Sightseeing

Agios Gerasimos Monastery

Location: Valsamata   The Monastery of Agios Gerasimos in Kefalonia, Ionian: Saint Gerasimos, born in 1503 in Trikala Thessaly, is the protector saint of Kefalonia. Saint Gerasimos was ordained a monk at Mount Athos, then went to Jerusalem where he lived for 12 years, passed to Crete and Zakynthos to finally arrives in Kefalonia where he died in August 15th, 1579. He was declared a saint in 1622. The first 5 years in Kefalonia, Agios Gerasimos lived in a cave in Lassi. This cave can be visited today and it has natural daylight and sea view. In 1560, Saint Gerasimos founded a nunnery in the valley of Omala, central Kefalonia, and called it the New Jerusalem

The monastery is situated under the imposing Mount Ainos and near the villages of Fragata and Valsamata. Today the monastery has been reconstructed. It is an imposing building with a newly built church. Beneath the monastery there is a cave with two rooms which used to be the home of the Saint. The only way to access this cave is by a large hole. The monastery is considered one of the most sacred pilgrimages in Kefalonia hosting a great number of visitors. A small church to Agios Gerasimos has been built above the tomb and the cave of the saint. The Saint also had planted a plane tree which is still preserved at the monastery. On his feast day, August 16th, there is a grand litany for the commemoration of the saint's death in which his sarcophagus is paraded and laid under the plane tree. Agios Gerasimos was known for his miraculous abilities to cure people with mental illnesses. His miracles which became widely known across the country, led to the removal of his relics that were found totally incorrupt. Today, his relics are saved in double glass reliquary placed above the saint's tomb.

Archaeological Museum

Ancient Acropolis

Location: Sami   The Ancient Acropolis of Sami, Kefalonia: Ancient Sami was a powerful fortified town whose ruins are found in Lapitha Mountain, over the port town of Sami Kefalonia. This town was an autonomous and independent state with its own coin inhabited from the Paleolithic Times. A strong and densely populated town with strong fortifications, it was located on top of the cliff. Several references of Ancient Sami are found in Homer's poems (Heliad, Odyssey) when Sami fought in the Trojan War. Though, in 188 B.C, Sami lost its autonomy and freedom during the siege from the Romans. During the Roman times, Ancient Sami flourished again due to the trade development and the increasing population. At that time, they built luxurious houses and public buildings. Excavations have brought to light parts of the citadel built during the Hellenistic Period and some Cyclopean walls situated in Paleokastro and Agioi Fanendes, from where the view is spectacular. The walls included 22 entrances, parts of an ancient theatre and rich tombs that date back to the 3rd century B.C. The view from Ancient Sami to the sea and the inland is great.

Cave of Agios Gerasimos

Location: Lassi   The Cave of Agios Gerasimos in Kefalonia, Ionian: On a hill above the tourist resort of Lassi, just 3 km from Argostoli, the capital of Kefalonia, visitors can see the Cave of Agios Gerasimos. This is the cave where Agios Gerasimos, the saint protector of the island, lived for five years, leading a strict ascetic life. Agios Gerasimos, originating from a noble family of northern Peloponnese, became a monk in Mount Athos and after visiting many places around Greece, he ended up in Kefalonia in 1555. He lived in this cave for 5 years, until 1560, when he went to the valley of Omala and rebuilt the Monastery of Panagia. This monastery was later called Monastery of Agios Gerasimos and it is today considered the protector of the island. In fact, on August 16th, on the name day of Agios Gerasimos, the most important religious festival takes place on the island. The Cave of Agios Gerasimos is very narrow and has a small hole from where you can get a great view over Lassi and the Ionian Sea. Next to the entrance of the cave, a small church has been built dedicated to the memory of the saint. Holy Masses are officiated in this church mostly on important religious celebrations.

Iakovatios Library

Location: Lixouri   Iakovatios Library and Museum of Kefalonia: One of the places of interest on the Greek island of Kefalonia is the Iakovatios Library and Museum. The library and museum is in the suburbs of Lixouri. The library is inside a pre-earthquake mansion that used to belong to the Typaldi-Iakovatios family. It was restored to its original grandeur in 1984. There are 20,000 books in this library displayed in 14 rooms with wood-paneled ceilings. One fifth of these books are from the 16th, 17th, 18th and 19th centuries. 7,000 of these books were originally owned by Iakovatios family. 5,000 books used to belong to a theology professor named Alivizatos. A book called The Complete Works of Hippocrates, published in 1595, is considered to be the most valuable book in this library.

The library-museum takes up one floor of the building. Other than books, it has a collection of documents belonging to the Iakovatios family, church vestments, antique furniture, the Metropolitan's bedroom suite, portraits, a 1954 leaden seal, a psalter in 4 languages, prelatic garments, bishop crosses and more. You can see 36 icons. The most notable of these icons are The Assembly of Archangels by Philotheos and To en Honais thayma by Damaskinos. These icons can be found in a special chamber. You can find three gospels from the Bible on parchments from the 10th, 14th and 15th centuries. The parchments are animal skins. The library also houses the 1556 edition of The Complete Works of Plato. This edition is from Venice. The library is surrounded by a beautiful garden. This museum is unique for its architecture and collection. You should definitely make this museum a part of your visit to Kefalonia

Castle of Saint George

Location: Peratata   The Venetian Castle of Saint George in Kefalonia: The Castle of Saint George is located 7 km south east of Argostoli, above the village Peratata Kefalonia. It has a polygonal shape and covers an area of 16,000 sq. m. This Castle was originally built in the 12th century by the Byzantines but it was mostly the Venetians who gave it its present form. In fact, its external walls were built in 1504 by the Venetians. The castle is ruined today and only a few buildings survive. It was not only the time and wars that caused its damages. This castle also suffered a lot from the earthquake that hit Kefalonia in 1956. At the time of its glory, inside the Castle, there were residences, public buildings, storehouses with food and guns, churches, hospitals, prisons, cisterns of water and generally an organized town. In fact, this Castle was the capital of Kefalonia before Argostoli was made the new capital in 1757. Close to a small square in the castle, you will also see the ruins of the Catholic Church of Saint Nicholas

Castle of Assos

Location: Assos   The Venetian Castle of Assos in Kefalonia: The Castle of Assos was built in the 16th century by the Venetians to protect the village from pirate attacks. Fortifications used to cover almost the entire village, though today not much of the Castle remains. Parts of the walls and an arched entrance gate are the mainly preserved sections. These remaining parts though have vivid the Venetian fortification style and the Venetian Lion of Saint Mark over the gates. The Castle of Assos had four entrance gates, but only two remain today. Within the ruins, you will find some interesting structures, such as the small church of Agios Markos and the house of the Venetian High Commissioner.

A little lower down the hill there is another chapel dedicated to Prophet Elias, which also contains a beautiful wooden carved iconostasis. The strategic location of the Castle allowed supervising the whole sea area and from there you can get beautiful view of the bay. Till 1956, the Castle of Assos was used as a place for political prisoners, who lived there and cultivated vineyards

De Bosset Bridge

Location: Argostoli   The De Bosset Bridge in Argostoli Kefalonia: The De Bosset Bridge or the De Bosset Causeway is the largest stone bridge on a sea water body and has been in existence since 1813, when the Swiss engineer Charles Philippe De Bosset was employed by the British Army. Thanks to his contribution in the form of study and construction of the bridge, Monsieur de Bosset was appointed as Governor of Kefalonia from 1810-1814 by the British who reigned the Ionian Islands from 1809-1864.

The town of Argostoli on the narrow Fanari peninsula projecting out from Argostoli Gulf was the nerve centre for all trade and commerce activities for the villagers in the island. But the inlet separated Argostoli from mainland Kefalonia unless you are traveling south and therefore, made it compulsory to travel around the perimeter of the 5 km long inlet. The British governors saw a strong local opposition when they drew plans to link the two sides of the inlet at its narrowest part by building a wooden bridge from the southern harbor side of Argostoli to Drapano, a small village 950 meters across the water. The to-be-solved transportation problems of the villagers allayed their fears about possible invasions and the De Bosset Bridge was completed in two weeks. The little strength of the bridge called for its remodeling in the year 1842. Baron Everton gave the bridge a new appearance and rebuilt it with stone using materials from the Metela hill. As you pass the bridge upon arrival in the island's capital, a four faced symmetrical obelisk made up of carved rocks rises from the sea.

This monument called Kolona existed since 1813 and was the Kefalonian Parliament's symbol of gratitude to Great Britain. The obelisk had a plaque in four languages: Greek, English, Italian and Latin with the inscription To the glory of the British Empire, which was mysteriously striken in 1865, when the Greeks regained control of the island. Since then, the inscription changed according to the different ruling periods. There used to exist a small walkway connecting the obelisk to the bridge but now it has disappeared.

The disastrous earthquake of 1953 injured one-third of the bridge on Argostoli side. The bridge and the obelisk survived the earthquake, but like the whole city, it required major restoration using modern concrete building methods. The bridge remained the boundary between the sea and Koutavos lagoon and periodically, several arches were added on the side of the bridge of Argostoli to impart additional strength to the bridge. Koutavos lagoon, created as result of the bridge, has become a breeding site for the Loggerhead turtles that favor the south end of the lagoon. The salt marshes and the shallow water have made the site a sanctuary for aquatic birds thriving on the resources available.

Further across the north end of the bridge, about 200 meters along the road to Dilinata the British cemetery of Kefalonia can be found, where over two hundred British Servicemen rest as well as their wives, children and a handful of civilians that had served Kefalonia as British servicemen or have called the place home. Increased advancements of technology and its easy availability had effects on the local traffic that comprehensively weakened the bridge to such an extent that it was closed in 2004 to all vehicles for extensive repair works.

The bridge was back in service in 2005, but with a few changes like a 2-tonne weight limit imposed upon cars and motorbikes and also, making the bridge a one-way route. So, you will have to drive around the lagoon at least once unless you are heading south. Plans to allow only pedestrian use of the bridge have been on the table for some time now to make the walk a little less stressful, but no matter what the decision is, the bridge still offers an excellent stroll preferably early in the evening.

Drogarati Cave

Location: Sami   The Drogarati Cave in Kefalonia: The Drogarati Cave in Kefalonia was discovered 300 years ago and opened to the public in 1963. It was discovered when a strong earthquake caused a collapse that revealed the cave's entrance. Drogarati is an impressive cave with remarkable formations of stalactites and stalagmites. Speleologists say that this cave is about 150 million years old and constitutes a rare geological phenomenon.The cave is about 60m deep and has a constant temperature of 18'1C. The humidity of the cave reaches 90%. Although it has undergone many damages because of earthquakes, stalactites still hang from the roof and form amazing shapes. As water drops fall onto these shapes and solidify, they give them another shape, long but gradually along centuries. Drogarati Cave consists of two parts. The part accessible to tourists consists of a long corridor that leads to the Royal Balcony, a natural platform of stalactites that beautifully reflect the light. From there, the visitor can see the Chamber of Exaltation, which has great acoustics. This chamber is the biggest hall of the cave; it is sometimes used to host cultural events and has a room for 500 people. To move from one part to the other, you cross colored columns and a small lake. Scientists have discovered that Drogarati cave has an extension that is not reachable and believe that, through this extension, it is connected to other sea caves. Drogarati Cave is therefore a natural art masterpiece that has taken its present form after thousands of years, while it continually changes. It is visited by lots of tourists every year and can be found 5 km to the south of Sami village, on the eastern coast of Kefalonia and right on the main road that connects Sami to Argostoli.:

Cyclopean Walls of Ancient Krani

Location: Argostoli   The Ancient Cyclopean Walls of Kefalonia Greece, Ionian: In Kefalonia there is a great site for the visitors of the island. It is the Cyclopean Walls, located near the former Doric temple of Demeter and some compare it to the Great Wall of China. They are called Cyclopean Walls because people indeed thought they were built by the one-eyed giants, the Cyclops. These Cyclopean walls are unfortunately in poor shape. Some of the walls have been destroyed and some others have been damaged by the elements. Acid rain had a detrimental effect on this wall over the years but many of them are still standing in good condition. Many people wonder how this wall can be so perfectly aligned. They were most likely built in 7th century BC. and claimed to be some of the best examples of engineering of walls coming from that time.

The way to go to the walls is pretty simple. They are near the main road that goes from Argostoli to Sami. When you get close to a village called Razata, you will see a sign that says Cylopean Walls. This sign points you to a asphalt road that eventually becomes a dirt road. There it happens to be a large open area to park your vehicle. You will have to walk the last remaining meters to these walls. When you visit, you'd better wear walking boots, strong sneakers or trainers as well as long pants or trousers to protect your legs from the prickly shrubs. These walls were meant to protect the ancient town of Krani. You can find remains of buildings from this town near the walls. The town used to be at the end of the Koutavos Bay and overlooked the whole region.

The Krania plain was the main location of this city. Krani was one of the cities of Kefalonia that were part of a kingdom called Ancient Sami that dominated Kelafonia for over three thousand years. The famous archeologist N. Kyparissis believes that the history of

Kefalonia is depicted in these walls. You can glimpse the ancient times right up to the years when the Roman Empire ruled this island. This time of period would be about three thousand years. The golden age of this island was during the Mycenean period. People were able to communicate with the islands of Ithaca, Lefkada and the Cycladic group of islands. All this communication ended when the island was destroyed by the volcanic eruption of Santorini. On a hill called Riza near these walls, there are many chamber tombs that existed before the Mycenaean period. Unfortunately, these tombs have been plundered and damaged. This hill was used as a necropolis for the ancient city of Krani. These cyclopean walls bear testimony to the fact that there was indeed ancient inhabitation on this island. These walls are over 2 kilometers long and can be found just outside Argostoli. While walking along these walls, you can see examples of the wildlife of the island. Despite their ruined state, the Cyclopean Walls og Kefalonia are a good example of ancient Greek engineering.

Katavothres

Location: Argostoli   Kefalonia Katavothres: On Kefalonia island there is a place that one should not miss visiting. This is one of the world's most astonishing geological phenomena for which there has been a lot of discussion. Katavothresis not dfficult to reach, as it takes only 3 kilometres from Argostoli long the Fanari road. The sea water rushes in through some cracks in the rocks on the shore and vanishes underground. In 1835, the phenomenon was rare enough that the English built some corn mills and while earthquakes broke the water wheel amazingly nothing happened to alter this trend of water coming in and going under. One could well ask where the wheel was set up so as to work.

They needed flowing water. This is where the rare geological formations came in to play. At Katavothres the sea flows inland and enters sinkholes on the earth that is below sea level. It is assumed that there are caverns below the seabed which is where the water flows in. The mills used to be run in these holes. The water would flow swiftly through the artificial channels and the wheel would start spinning. In 1963, Austrian geomorphologists added some purple dye to the water and followed its course only to make some surprising discoveries. It traveled in underground rivers then mixed with rainwater and finally reached the Melissani Lake almost fifteen kilometers away in its semi-salted form. From there the water flowed in to the sea at the village of Karavomilos, and all in all it had taken the purple water two weeks to make this trip across the island.

There is a cave at Melissani and this cave has lost its roof over a period of time to the severe earthquakes that have occurred. Now a lake has formed there which we know as the Melissani Lake and at the deepest point it is thirty-two meters deep. The lake has clear blue green water and the shades change throughout the day. Now the purple dye experiment revealed that the water that disappeared at Katavothres in Argosoli came out at the village of Karavomilos, and went on to form an almost circular fresh water lake, which then empties into the sea at Sami bay. The seawater is continuously falling in to these sink holes only to disappear.

One theory as to where the water might go is the theory propounded by Mousson. According to him the source of the movement was attributed to volcanic activity underground that heats the water. Since warm water has a lower specific weight and bigger volume than cold water, it would move up to the surface and this could explain the disappearance. But since there were no thermal springs in this area, these theories had some anomalies. There are a lot of other theories that have been circulated since but none can be unquestionably substantiated. A good idea is to go to Katavothres, enjoy the amazing sites and leave the questions as those known only to nature. There is a quaint village and a small shingle beach where one can relax and enjoy the earth's gift to mankind.

Lighthouse of Saint Theodoroi

Location: Argostoli   The lighthouse of Saint Theodoroi in Argostoli Kefalonia: The lighthouse of Saint Theodoroi lies on a man-made peninsula close to Argostoli village, the capital of the island. It is a circular structure with 20 columns and its tower is 8 m tall. The building has a rather simple and Doric architectural style, while its focal plane is 11 m. It was originally built in 1828 by the British administrator Charles Napier, who ruled the island that time.

Altough the British military rule was quite severe, they built important works that contributed in the prosperity of Kefalonia. In 1863, after the integration of the island to the Greek State, this lighthouse was included in the lighthouse network of Greece. The earthquake of 1953 was pretty devastating for Kefalonia and the other Ionian islands and also destroyed the lighthouse. It was rebuilt in 1960 by the local architect Takis Pavlatos according to its original architectural design. The lighthouse of Saint Theodoroi works till today and gives a romantic view at night. It is found 3 km from Argostoli, close to Katavothres, or you will see it if you take the boat to Lixouri village

Melissani Cave

Location: Sami   The Cave of Melissani in Kefalonia: Situated just outside Sami, the Cave of Melissani has a strange appeal. It is one of the most significant places for tourists to visit in Greece. Surprisingly, there is a lake inside the cave that has trees and forests surrounding it. The cave itself is B-shaped with two chambers or halls separated with land or an island in the center. The roof of one of the halls caved in centuries ago letting sunlight filter in. The depth of the lake is 20 to 30 meters.

When the sun is right overhead at noon, the sunlight hitting the turquoise-blue waters create a magical illusion and the whole Cave of Melissani suddenly feels lit with blue light. This is the best time to visit this cave. Slanting rays in the morning and evening have magical quality of their own. One gets an ethereal feeling of boats hovering in the light! Myth has it that the cave was named after the nymph Melissanthi who committed suicide because her love for God Pan was not reciprocated.

The excavations carried out in 1951 and later in 1962 many artifacts that were found dated to the 3rd and 4th century BC that were used during the post classical and early Hellenistic periods. Figures of nymphs unearthed have given credence to this legend.Small boats ply on the lake inside the Cave of Melissani. The cave is 36m high, 40m wide and 3.5 m long. A balcony was built on top of the cave for tourists to get a spectacular view of the inside from the top. The first chamber is sun-lit and the second chamber is dark and has many stalactites covered with algae and moss. Even though they are big in size, they are dwarfed by the huge dome. Surprisingly, many of the stalactites resemble dolphins, the companions and messengers of the nymphs as the legend goes.

This chamber is lit with electric lights. The water in the lake is a mixture of fresh water and seawater. It is about 500m away from the sea and the water is higher than the sea level by 1m. The brackish water enters the Cave of Melissani from one end and flows out from the other. Water is replenished by the springs gushing underneath the 30m in depth water inside.The Cave of Melissani leaves a memorable and lasting impression to everyone who visits it

Monastery of Argilion

Location: Sami   The Monastery of Argilion in Kefalonia, Greece: On a hill just above the bay of Sami, there is the Monastery of Agrilion, an important religious site for the locals. The location of the monastery offers incredible view to the blue green waters of Antisamos beach on one side and the towns of Sami and Agia Efimia on the other. The monastery was founded in the 18th century by two shepherds, who had found a miracle-working icon of Virgin Mary on that same spot in 1722.

These two shepherds, Jacob and Symeon, became monks and were the first monks to live in his monastery. It is said that Saint Cosmas of Aetolia (1700-1779), also known as Father Kosmas Etolos, an Orthodox monk and important figure of the Greek Enlightenment, stayed in this monastery during his visit on Kefalonia. The icon of Virgin Mary that was found by the two monks has been incorporated today in a larger icon of Virgin Mary (Panagia) Agriliotissa. There is a large panigiri in this monastery on August 15th, while the memory of Kosmas Etolos is also honored on August 24th

Monastery of Agios Andreas

Location: Peratata   The Monastery of Agios Andreas in Kefalonia: The monastery named after Apostle Andrew was founded during the Byzantine era but was reestablished in 1579 when Apostle Andrew started a small nunnery at this place. It was then privately owned by three spiritual sisters, Benedict, Leondia and Magdalen. The monastery received a large amount of money in 1630 from the Greek Romanian princess, Roxanne, who later was renamed Romila, to live the life of a nun. If Roxanne's treasure contributed to the reconstruction of the monastery, the spiritual treasure of Mount Athos further glorified the place.

The monastery is located at Milapedia in Peratata. The British and the nuns had a troublesome acquaintance during the early 19th century as the British seldom interrupted the divine services at the monastery. In the year 1832, the monastery's beautiful frescoes were covered with asbestos by the British as a sign of their fury at constant non-abiding attitude of the monastery. In this nunnery, a weekly Holy Mass takes place on Sunday, though solemn vigils are performed regularly. The nuns participate in making bishops' officiating robes, handicrafts and gardening. The celebrations at the nunnery take place on the Friday after Easter and on the feast day of Saint Apostle Andrew on the 30th of November.

The monastery has an associated church located in the old Katholikon of the nunnery and is the only building surviving from the monstrous earthquake of 1953. The major attraction in the 1988 established museum by the then Metropolite Spyridon are the Holy remains of the right foot (sole) of Apostle Andrew. The museum has treasures belonging to 1300-1900 AD and includes belongings from the abandoned churches of Kefalonia as well. Some of the valuable treasures to be seen at the museum include:

Agios Panagis or Priest Basia's shirt; two handwritten epistles from Agios Kosmas Aetolos dated to 1777; the Archiepiscopal sakkos embroidered by the Nun Theodora Kanali from Metaxata in the years between 1715 and 1721; the hieratic sceptre and the Communion Cup (Pastoral Staff and Chalice) of his Holiness Nicodemos II Metaxas and Archbishop of Kefalonia, the founder of the first Greek printing press in Constantinople in the 17th century; and the Shroud of the National Martyr and Patriarch of Constantinople Gregorios the fifth.

Among other display pieces are wall paintings, icons and frescoes from the church of Milapedia. Of special mention is the painting of the nun Romila with her parents. Also on display are the handworks of nun Romila, which are masterpieces because of the finely sewn golden embroidery

Monastery of Lagouvarda

Location: Markopoulo   The Church of Panagia Lagouvarda (Lady of the Snakes) in Markopoulo, Kefalonia: The Church of Panagia Lagouvarda is one of the most important churches in Kefalonia. Located in the historical village of Markopoulo, 30 km from Argostoli, in southern Kefalonia, this church is constructed on the site of an older monastery. The church was burnt down in 1945 and later it was totally destroyed by the severe earthquake of 1953. The special thing about this church is that every August snakes appear in the church yard. The locals say that they appear every year on August 6th and disappear on August 15th. These snakes are long and have the sign of a black cross on their heads and tongues. They do not harm people and the locals touch them for good luck.

Tradition says that the appearance of these snakes is a miracle of Virgin Mary since many centuries ago. In the Medieval times, while the pirates were trying to invade the monastery, the nuns prayed to Virgin Mary to save them and Virgin Mary turned them into snakes. When the pirates entered the monastery, the only found snakes on the floor and the yard of the church. Since them these snakes appear every August and this is why they also call the Monastery of Lagouvarda as the Lady of the Snakes. In fact, they consider it a bad sign if the snakes do not make their appearance one summer. It is said that the snakes did not appear only twice, before two fatal events for the island: in 1940 before World War II breaks in Greece and in 1953 before the strong earthquake that destroyed Kefalonia.

Monastery of Kipoureon

Location: Kaminarata   The Monastery of Kipoureon in Kefalonia: The Monastery of Kipoureon is located in the peninsula of Paliki, 15 km from Lixouri. The location of this monastery is amazing, as it has been constructed on top of a rock, 90 metres above the sea. The view to the Ionian Sea and the wild coastline is magnificent, which makes it a sight worth visiting if you are in the area. The Monastery of Kipoureon was founded in the 17th century by the Archibishop of Paxi Chrysanthos Petropoulos. Its name literally means monastery of the gardens due to the many gardens that the monks once cultivated to make their living. Today only one monk lives in the Monastery of Kipoureon, who welcomes visitors every day. Dedicated to the Holy Cross and the Annunciation of the Virgin, the monastery celebrates on March 25th and September 14th. Inside there is a wonderful collection of ecclesiastical relics and post-Byzantine icons. The natural surrounding of the monastery is lush green and comprises of pine trees and fur trees. From the yard, visitors can enjoy a wonderful sunset to the Ionian Sea.

Monastery of Panagia Atros

Location: Poros   The Monastery of Panagia Atrou in Kefalonia: The monastery of Atros is a survivor. The monastery was destroyed 17 times mostly due to earthquakes and fires. But every time it was damaged, the monks built it again. The monastery has caught the fancy of the Saracens in the past as they attacked it thrice during the Middle Ages costing the lives of 127 monks. Then, the actual fortress was built at the monastery to protect the monks and their belongings and valuables. The oldest monastery of Kefalonia, the monastery of Atros, is located on the triangular hill, Mt. Atros at an altitude of 760 meters above sea level. It is situated 5 kms away from the town of Poros. This monastery, built in the Byzantine era in the 8th century, holds both cultural and historical importance.

The monastery is also known as Theotokos Monastery and is dedicated to the birth of Virgin Mary. The monastery still preserves a medieval tower along with the archodariki and the Welcome Hall. Agios Clemes led his ascetic life at the monastery. The earliest reference to the monastery is by the Latin Archbishop of Kefalonia in his 1248 report. The monastery celebrates the feast of Virgin's birth on September 8th, which is inaugurated by an evening service on the previous day. Although new monastic quarters had been, at present, only one monk lives in the monastery. It is a perfect destination for both adventure-seekers interested in going off the beaten track or couples looking for a romantic walk. The climb to the monastery offers some magnificent views of Poros and its harbor. Of special mention is the sunrise at the monastery

Monastery of Sissia

Location: Lourdas   The Monastery of Sissia in Kefalonia, Ionian: The Monastery of Virgin Mary of Sissia stands on a hill above Lourdas Beach, Kefalonia. Tradition says that this monastery was founded in the 13th century by Saint Francis of Assisi, the Catholic saint protector of animals, birds and all species of nature. This is probably how the name of the monastery derived, by its founder. In the Medieval times, this was a very wealthy monastery and its frescoes and icons were painted by famous iconographers. In particular, the monastery was so important that in 1676 the Venetians introduced an annual march from Sissia to the Castle of Saint George in Peratata Kefalonia to celebrate the feast of Saint Mark. Gradually the monastery from Catholic became Orthodox. In 1953, the strong earthquake that hit the Ionian islands completely destroyed the monastery. A new building was constructed on a spot near the old monastery that now lays in ruins.

Monastery of Themata

Location: Agia Efimia   The Monastery of Themata in Kefalonia, Ionian: Located on the slopes of Agia Dinati Mountain, the Monastery of Panagia Themata is one of the oldest monuments of Kefalonia, dating back to 1096. There are many assumptions in how the monastery got its name. Some people believe that there was an old settlement named Themata in the region that gave its name to the monastery. Other believe that this monastery was the seat of an bishop in the Byzantine times, when Kefalonia was a thema (Byzantine administrative unit).

The monastery is located about 9 km from Agia Efimia, high in the mountains surrounded by a large pine forest. Actually, it is one of the best trekking paths along the mountain of Agia Dinati, offering an amazing view to the east shores of Kefalonia and Ithaca. The Monastery of Panagia Themata celebrates twice a year, on August 15th and the first Tuesday after Easter. In fact, this Tuesday, there is a large celebration with a litany of the holy icon of Panagia, dancing of local groups and a panigiri in the pine forest

Kefalonia wildlife

Kefalonia, the largest island of the Ionian Sea, is considered one of the most beautiful Greek islands for the richness, variety and harmony of its natural beauties. A perfect mix of sea, beaches, mountains, verdant plains, flora and fauna. The island is ideal for a direct contact with nature, in the sense of both naturism and nudism!

The coast of Kefalonia is quite varied, offering powerful contrasting landscapes. Stretches of sandy beaches on shallow crystal waters, white pebbles, large and small creeks (many still unexplored) offering the best Greek beaches, among the best in the world. Just to remember few of them: Myrtos Beach and the beautiful natural surroundings of Skala, Antìsamos, Makrìs Yalòs, Xi, Ammes, Avithos, Lourdàs and Koutsoupià. Furthermore, there are also naturist beaches in Kefalonia, including: Agios Sissios - Antisamos - Trapezaki - Koroni - Platia Ammos.

The mountainous highlands dominate all the other Ionian islands extending from Cape Dafnoudi to the extreme south of Cape Mounda, where we find the most important mountain called Enos. The few and small plains of the island are in the area of Krania, Omalon, Sami, Pilarou, Livathou and Palikis.

Mount Enos reaches, to the highest peak (Soros), the altitude of 1628 meters thus being the second heighest mountain on Greek islands. It is also one of the ten National Greek Parks, a refuge for migratory birds and mammals, the ideal habitat for rare species of flowers, shrubs and herbs. Its slopes are covered with trees of a dark green species that grows only here (abies cephalonica).

The Kefalonia Fir Tree
There was a time when Mount Enos was rich in forests of Kefalonia Abies, the Kefalonia fir, which grows above 800 meters. At a glance it looks like a black forest, with dark green leaves, which led the

Venetians to call the Ainos mountain chain "Black Mountain". The forest still exists, but it has been devastated over the centuries by the timber trade and the forest fires. This tree is endemic to the area, but it can be also found on most of southern greek hills. From this tree it can obtained a very valuable wood, that was highly demanded to build the old wooden ships. No coincidence that the columns of Knossos in Crete were created by the fir trees of Kefalonia. Over the centuries, the timber trade from Kefalonia has been intesified, thanks to the fact that the woods of firs were accessible and close to the sea, and then easily shipped. In addition, also forest fires have played a significant role in devastating these forests. In 1962 the area was declared a National Park in order to protect this species of fir trees, of which islanders are proud of.

The shape and the limestone stratification of Kefalonia determines the presence of important geological phenomena all over the island (such as the corrosion of the limestone that gives life to caves, abysses, etc.). Particularly interesting are the caves of Melissani Agalaki, Saint Theodoron, Zervati, Drogarati, Sakou. These geological phenomena are are very interesting especially with regard to the behavior of waters. Not by chance that Kefalonia has been called the island of the "bizarre", because of its numerous and unusual natural phenomena, such as moving rocks, waters that disappear, strange flowers and more.

The Katavothres (or Thalassomilos) is a rare geological phenomenon for which the sea water pours through the cracks in the rocks near the shore and disappears underground. Also known as the phenomenon of "sinking holes", the Katavothres can be observed at 2.5 km from Argostoli, near the sea mills, whose carsic holes swallow the water that disappears into the ground. The research revealed that the same water that disappears at Katavothres in Argostoli, flows near the village of Karavomilos at Sami, forming an almost circular lake of fresh water, then flowing into the sea in the bay of Sami.

In the Melissani Cave the most part of the roof has collapsed throughout the years because of the numerous earthquakes (the last one in 1953) creating a slope so that waters of Karavomilos form a large lake in the cave. In its deepest point, Lake Karavomilos is 32 meters deep and is well know for its crystal clear waters and the changing shades of blue and green that can be observed in different moments of the day.

Another geological phenomenon is called Kounopetra (the moving stone). It is a large monolithic rock with a circumference of 20 meters that juts out into the sea. It is located in the western part of the island at Paliki, near the village of Manzavinata. The phenomenon, unique in the world, consists of a rhythmic and continuous movement of the rock, from east to west, about 20 times per minute. The phenomenon, visible from the sea or while standing on the rock, has weakened in the lsat decades until the earthquake of 1953 that has slipped the rock providing stability.

The Flora
Flowers abound in Kefalonia, especially in the spring, from the omnipresent brooms to the poenie and some rare species of wild orchids, but the best time to see them is from late March to April and May, although the season lasts longer in the upper part of Mount Ainos. This area of the mountain, now protected as national park, offers a great variety of protected species like the endemic fir, Abies Cephalonia. The orchids stand out in the spring in about 31 different species. Despite the heat and lack of water during the summer, there are always flowers to observe, like the beautiful marine Narcissus (Pancratium maritimum) and the mullein. Autumn rains give vigorous life to the crocus and to the cyclamen with a new flush of long lasting flowers, coloring the winter until the arrival of spring.

The Fauna

The fauna is surprisingly rich here and the island has a variety of wildlife including foxes, hares, weasels, martens and hedgehogs. The latter is most likely to be met so that people sometimes can not cross the road safely. Wild horses are common on the sides of Mount Ainos, but the sightings are rare. The land turtles are too many and they are often seen on the side of the road. Snakes are also very numerous, but they are mostly harmless. A rare and protected species of seals live on the rugged and inaccessible shores of the island. Of particular note are two phenomena affecting animals of the island. Near the mountain "Agia Dynati" some goats and rabbits have golden or silver teeth, because of the composition of the soil. Another rarity is about the goats on the island - according to the historian Claudio Eliano, goats could survive without water for six months, only living of the moisture fo the breeze. This has been confirmed by modern pastors.

The Monk Seal
The sea between Kefalonia and Ithaca appears to be the natural habitat of the rare monk seal, in danger of extinction, and that thrives in the warm waters of the Mediterranean and the Atlantic, off the coast of North Africa. Mentioned by Homer, seals were far more prolific in the ancient world, losing in the last centuries the classic breeding habits and being repeatedly threatened by

fishermen. This rare and shy animal shelters in caves and remote places to hide from men and to give birth to a seal pup (that is usually just one puppy). The development of tourism along the coast and the increasing leisure activities around the sea shores have seriously interfered with the usual gatherings of the species. The monk seal lives of fish and octopus, but the progressive scarcity of food led to serious conflicts with fishermen. Too many times in the past, the conflict was resolved by simply killing the seals, especially when it was accidentally trapped in the nets. Now the focus is on the conservation of the species with many active groups supporting the project to protect the small population of seals that live around Cephalonia, Ithaca and Lefkada.

Caretta-Caretta

The Caretta-Caretta (or Caretta turtle) is a rare sea turtle that lives in the Mediterranean Sea, and particularly along the coasts of Kefalonia and Zakynthos. They can grow to considerable size, with a weight up to 140 kg. Despite their size, these turtles can swim very fast, thanks to their large and rigid flippers on the front and to the rear. However, on the mainland they become extremely vulnerable and slow because, unlike other turtles, the Caretta-Caretta turtle can not retract into its carapace to hide.

Caretta-Caretta turtles always breed on the same beach where they were born, and for this reason it is important that the nesting beach is kept as untouched as possible. The nesting period is from June to August, when the female of the species makes its way to the beach to lay eggs. The female explores the land by controlling the distance from the sea, the temperature and quality of the sand, in order to choose a suitable place to lay eggs. Once the choice is made the turtle digs with its fins a couple of feet deep hole, where to lay its eggs. Eggs are small and soft and do not break when dropped into the hole. The nest contains about 120 eggs that hatch usually 50 days after the laying. Eggs are protected by the sand and kept warm by the sun. Usually about 60% of all eggs hatch and young turtles move towards the sea following the horizon and the refelction of the moonlight on sea. Only a small percentage survive - the physical obstacles on the beach and the lights of restaurants and bars often confuse young turtles. Once in the water the little turtle will meet even greater dangers with only one in a thousand that will reach adulthood. Some of the beaches of Kefalonia are highly protected during the breeding season of the turtle, including Mounda Beach near Skala, Trapeazaki Beach, Minies Beach and the area near the airport. There is a non-profit organization based in Katelios that works to preserve this species in danger of extinction.

Kefalonia villages

Kefalonia is by extension the fifth largest island in Greece, after Rhodes, Lesbos, Crete and Evia. Kefalonia has an international airport with lots of direct flights, especially charters, from many european countries. If you are traveling to Kefalonia is obviously easier to go by plane directly there, but you can also fly to Athens, Preveza (near Lefkada) or Zante and continue the journey with a domestic flight (Athens), bus (Athens and Preveza to Lefkada) or ferry (Lefkada and Zakynthos).

Kefalonia has twelve villages with more than 500 residents, in addition there are many small villages. The island's capital is Argostoli, that is also the administrative, financial and cultural center.

Most of the villages of Kefalonia were hit by a strong earthquake in 1953, which destroyed many houses and public buildings. The only village that was not touched by the earthquake is Fiscardo, on the north side of the island, standing out for its colored walls and the picturesque harbor.

Argostoli: The largest town on the island with its 9,000 inhabitants is the capital, the financial and the administrative center of the island. Mostly it is a town for the locals with few tourists, made of simple shops and trendy cafes on Lithostrato (the "stone street"), the only paved road of the nineteenth century with walking paths, reserved for pedestrians.

Founded in 1757 by the Venetians, Argostoli lost its characteristic traditional face after the earthquake of 1953. Around the daily market, on the shores of the gulf, the atmosphere looks like that of the 50s with simple and traditional buildings.

A vague elegance is instead found in Platia Valianou square, the center of the walk after dinner.

Argostoli extends over 2 km on the east bank of the peninsula of Lasi. Reinforced concrete buildings and old houses covered in red bricks stand on the low hill, while on the opposite side there are lots of tourist resorts and the nice beaches of Lasi.

The long and narrow gulf which separates the peninsula from the center of the island and making Argostoli look like a town on a lake, is crossed by the road Drapano, built by the British in 1812. Nowadays the footbridge is so fragile that it can be crossed only by pedestrians, cyclists and fishermen. Landmarks in Argostoli: Archaeological Museum - The Library of Korgialenios - Agios Spiridonas Napier's Park - Seawater Mills - The Lighthouse- The War

Memorial.Beaches near Argostoli: Makris Gialos beach - Platis Gialos beach - Tourkopodero

Lixouri: Second largest town, in the past, Lixouri was the most important port of Kefalonia and the headquarters of the Venetians.

After the returning of migrants to the country and thanks to many students, Lixouri has been extremly modernized. Several new buildings have been built with the many European funding. The center is the platia, the cobbled square with the impressive ficus near the new theater.

By car you can discover the Paliki peninsula: first the beaches to the south, then across the mountains to the steep coast to the west, where the monastery of Kipourion stands out. Landmarks in Lixouri: Iakovatos Museum - The Monastery of Kipouria.Beaches near Lixouri: Xi beach - Vatsa beach - Platia Ammos beach - Livadi beach - Petani beach

Assos: Beyond the mountain village of Divarata, where the peninsula Erissos starts, a winding road rises snaking up the hill. Down below is the small peninsula of Asos, reached by a blind street that cuts through the many hills full of young cypress trees, proving how the intensive agriculture has characterized the past of the island.

In the late sixteenth century the whole peninsula was walled by the Venetians, in order to create a fortress to protect the inhabitants from the attack of enemies. In front of the peninsula stands the village of Assos, at the end of a narrow inlet.

Although the beach is short and stony, the resort attracts many tourists due to the atmosphere that reigns in the cafes and taverns of the "square of Paris." The square was so called because the city of Paris had given consistent and effective aid to the people of this village, almost completely destroyed by the earthquake of '53. In fact, walking around the country you can still find many ruined old houses. Landmarks in Assos: The Castle Beaches near Assos: Myrtos beach

Fiskardo: Mostly part spared by the disaster of 1953, Fiscardo has remained the most idyllic corner of the island. The many yachts that dock here in the summer give the village a sort of wellness, as evidenced by all the colorful houses, recently renovated and "rejuvenated".

Pines, olive trees and cypresses surround Fiscardo, and the walk to the harbour is forbidden to cars. You can swim from both the flat rocks along the harbour bay, and on the nearby pebbled beaches that can be reached on foot in 20 minutes.

The town's name derives from the Norman leader Robert Guiscard, who made several raids in the Ionian Islands and who was struck by the plague in 1085 as he was about to attack again. Landmarks in Fiskardo: Norman Ruins. Beaches near Fiskardo: Dafnoudi beach

Sami: Sami is home to the main port of the island of Kefalonia, but it is not a resort destination. Thanks to the campsite and the long pebble beach, however, there are small groups of young tourists. Some sites of cultural interest close to Sami, however, make it an attractive destination for those who want to go hiking. Landmarks in Sami: Ancient Sami - Melissani Cave - Drogarati Cave Beaches near Sami: Andisamos beach - Melissani Lake

Kastro: Despite its beauty, Kastro has remained a quiet town. It lies on a hill above the plain of Livathos up to a Venetian fortress built in the sixteenth century, and which is visible from Argostoli. The houses of the village are small, old and modest, but well-kept. Here still live the natives. Landmarks in Kastro: Monastery of Agios Gerassimos - Fortress of Agios Georgios

Livatho: Particularly fertile strip of land, the coastal area around Leivathos has 25 well-kept villages full of flowers, including Metaxata, Svoronata, Domata, Kourkoumelata and Minia. Landmarks in Livatho: Monastery of Agios Andreas Milapidias -

Mycenaean tombs of Mazarakata (Tafi Mazarakaton) Beaches near Livatho: Porto Heli beach - Avithos beach - Ligia beach - Trapezaki beach

Skala: Completely rebuilt after the earthquake of 1953, Skala is a nice resort much loved especially by the British, with a long sandy beach with dunes and a small woodland right on the seashore. The remains of a Roman villa testify to the presence of an ancient settlement. Landmarks in Skala: Roman villa. Beaches near Skala: Kaminia beach - Koroni beach

Poros: Situated between a long pebble beach and a small ferry port, Poros extends for 2 km along the coast. Unlike Skala, the city is quiet and not crowded yet, on the other hand is not particularly attractive.Landmarks in Poros: Monastery of Theotokou Atrou - Mycenaean tomb of Tzanata (Tafi Tzanaton)

Peratata: Peratata is a small village located 8 km south-east of Argostoli. Built on a hillside of Mount Ainos and surrounded by a verdant landscape, Peratata offers a relaxing stay to its visitors. The houses are made of stone and there are picturesque alleyways leading to various monuments spread throughout the region. The Castle of St. George is located on the hill overlooking the village.

www.ingramcontent.com/pod-product-compliance
Lightning Source LLC
Chambersburg PA
CBHW021100080526
44587CB00010B/314